Intimacy

Also by Ziyad Marar and published by Acumen

Deception

Intimacy

Understanding the Subtle Power of Human Connection

Ziyad Marar

ACUMEN

First published in 2012 by Acumen

Acumen Publishing Limited

4 Saddler Street
Durham
DH1 3NP, UK

ISD, 70 Enterprise Drive
Bristol, CT 06010, USA

www.acumenpublishing.com

ISBN: 978-1-84465-527-4

British Library Cataloguing-in-Publication Data
A catalogue record for this book is available from the British Library.

Typeset in Warnock Pro.
Printed and bound in the UK by MPG Books Group.

For Kate, Anna, Ellie and Charlotte

Contents

Acknowledgements ix

1. Only Connect 1

2. Translating Intimacy 15

3. The Kiss 33

PART ONE Intimacy Through Four Lenses

4. It Takes Two 49

5. A Conspiracy 65

6. Unruly Emotion 81

7. A Complicated Kindness 103

CONTENTS

PART TWO Barriers to Intimacy

8. Insecurities   123

9. Solipsism and Imaginative Failures   135

10. Wishful Thinking   149

11. Cultures and Contexts   165

PART THREE Finding Intimacy

12. Learning from Literature   189

13. In Good Faith   209

Bibliography   217
Index   221

Acknowledgements

I'm grateful to many people whose conversation has influenced and stimulated my thinking about intimacy over the years.

Geoff Lattimer has been an encouraging enthusiast for this topic since the writing began and throughout the process, and was also there at the end to comment insightfully on the final draft. Along the way I was lucky to have helpful reading and comments from Sarah Brierly, Kate Buchanan, Dave Clarke, Daniel Crewe, Will Francis, Leith Marar, Nael Marar and Dave Stephenson.

Since I started this book Food Club (aka Fight Club) has provided a regular backdrop: a space to discuss and to disagree about, and often to find, intimacy. Thanks to Jamilah Ahmed, Michael Carmichael, Zoë Elliott-Fawcett, Miranda Nunhofer, Caroline Porter and Lucy Robinson for stimulating discussion and debate and particular thanks to those clubbers who also went as far as to read and comment on part or all of the script Robert Rojek, Dave Ross, and Kiren Shoman.

Acumen has provided a natural home for me. Kate Williams's rigorous editing has been exemplary, and special thanks are due to Steven Gerrard, whose critical eye and deep interest in the topic made the whole publishing experience an instructive pleasure. I am also very grateful to Nigel Warburton whose careful and perceptive reading improved the final script in many ways.

I'm most grateful of all to my wife, Kate Buchanan, who provided the space, time and loving support that enabled this book to grow in the midst of our crowded lives. And to our daughters Anna, Ellie and Charlotte for allowing holidays, weekends and many a conversation to be infiltrated by this project.

Finally, I have dedicated this book to my family, each of whom, in the latter stages of writing, supported one another at a time when Kate's diagnosis and thankfully successful treatment for breast cancer taught us all more than we needed to know about the preciousness of human connection.

1

Only Connect

Contemporary society discourages intimacy. We live in a self-regarding culture, soaked through with the impersonal need for instant gratification. Our goal is to get intimate with ourselves rather than others, to identify and indulge in our own desires and fantasies (where do you want to go today?) and to satisfy them by consuming the right products. Success and the pursuit of status are trumpeted at the expense of human connection.

Alongside the rise and rise of consumer culture we've experienced a technological revolution that replaces intimacy with simulation. The age of the internet has made us all feel more connected and yet, paradoxically, more distant. Books about connection emphasize the networks of "weak ties" in which we are all immersed and the need we have to plug in and play. With so many relationships now mediated through screens we are beginning to appreciate the limitations of digital interactions as well as the virtues. As with our attitudes to that vanishing commodity, the physical book, we are treasuring those moments of face-to-face interaction with real people in actual rather than virtual environments.

On the other hand, the dominant rhetoric in the media is one of intimacy. The yin of a consumer culture plays against the yang of a therapeutic one. Songs, films and literature are forever reminding us to overcome our shallower desires and guilty pleasures and repeat the (supposed?) "wisdom" that love conquers all. Now, more than at any other time in human history, the hope to find deep and mutual understanding through intimacy with another person is a dominant ambition that permeates the whole of our culture. E. M. Forster distilled it with a simple instruction: "only connect".

Of course it is not so simple. Intimacy is elusive, subtle and often short-lived even when found. But before we explore our hopes for and the many barriers to intimacy let us look closely at an informative example. Sofia Coppola's film *Lost in Translation*, trading on a cinematic trope familiar since *Brief Encounter*, illustrates the beguiling power of an intimate connection quite beautifully.

Bill Murray plays Bob Harris, a physically and spiritually exhausted actor in the twilight of his career. Bob has come to Tokyo, overcoming his self-loathing, to do a lucrative commercial for Japanese whisky. He tries to follow hectoring instructions, in badly translated Japanese, to pull off a Roger Moore pout to camera (not Sean Connery to his chagrin) and to growl "for relaxing times ... make it Suntory time". Scarlett

Charlotte and Bob, in *Lost in Translation* (dir. Sofia Coppola, 2003).

Johansson plays Charlotte, the philosophy graduate from Yale who is along for the ride with her narcissistic photographer husband, John, also in Tokyo to do a shoot for a rock band. He is constantly at work and leaves her to kill solitary time in their hotel room. Bob is in his fifties, Charlotte is in her twenties: both disorientated, depressed and sleepless in Tokyo.

Unencumbered by the baggage, history and shared projects that limit rather than enhance the relationships they have with their spouses, Bob and Charlotte find solace and more in each other. Both have reasons to run towards each other; one in a marriage only two years old but suffering from neglect, the other in a marriage that after twenty-five years is ground down by habit, leaving the couple wearily at odds with each other. The obscurity of Bob's past is the counterpoint to the obscurity of Charlotte's future.

Their hotel in particular and the city in general provide the backdrop; neon garishness and constant noise, compounded by their inability to speak the local language, reinforce the lack of human connection. Nor can their sense of alienation be reversed by making contact with loved ones. While the implication of modern travel is that "home" is always a phone call or a fax message (or now an email) away, any long-distance relationship is plagued by mistranslation of its own. On the phone to his wife in Los Angeles, Bob tells her about places he has been going to and the people he has been meeting. She comments, "I'm glad you're having fun", to which he quickly replies, "It's not fun. It's just very, very different".

"Do I need to worry about you, Bob?"
"Only if you want to."

She sends him urgent faxes about fabric samples she has sent him in order to decorate his study, which couldn't be further from his current preoccupations. "I love the burgundy", he lurches while the camera pans across a few barely distinguishable samples piled on the floor.

He confesses at one point that he is "completely lost" then brightens with the idea that he wants to look after his health and that he no longer wants "all that pasta". He wants instead to "start eating … Japanese food", to which she caustically replies, "Well, why don't you just stay there and you can have it every day?"

Charlotte also tries for a long-distance connection by ringing her close friend back in Los Angeles. She complains that after visiting a shrine "I didn't feel anything". Then she blurts out, "I don't know who I married". The conversation founders as Charlotte cannot communicate her disarray to her friend. The friend assumes that Charlotte is simply lucky to be on holiday and away from the humdrum world of normality. Meanwhile her husband, while near at hand, is absent through his focus on his work and on an alarmingly self-regarding and shallow celebrity called Kelly (played by Anna Faris) who happens to be staying at the same hotel, and over whom he slavers.

Against this disorientating and harsh background Bob and Charlotte create a small and subtle interplay that is all the more powerful for being understated. They make knowing eye contact across crowded bars, share private jokes at onlookers' expense, go into the city together and slowly gravitate to each other. In each other they find a temporary haven, a quiet sense of home. It is important that as much passes between them in their gaze as in words. This near telepathic mutual understanding serves only to heighten the sense of conspiracy, reducing everyone else to a farcical backdrop. While the emotion between them is clearly heightened, it is faintly drawn. Too florid an emotional display would have created a barrier, too obvious a path a dead end to intimate knowledge.

The elusiveness of intimacy

Today we live with a deep ambivalence about other people: we should not let them hold us back, and yet "love is the only law". Reconciling those two attitudes is not straightforward. In my book *The Happiness Paradox* I describe this modern consciousness as torn by contradictory demands: on the one hand to escape from others who may have too much power over our lives, our potent audiences (to be authentic and free), and on the other to embrace them (to belong, to feel justified, to be valued). We want to connect with others without losing our autonomy and to express our freedom without being isolated. The relationship between these needs is paradoxical because the expression of one conjures up the need for its counterpart. As we turn our backs on those who would shape our lives we risk alienation or narcissism and must face them again, and as we face them we risk submergence and neediness, and so must be prepared to turn away; we are in a perpetual oscillation when it comes to other people. We want to be with them and influenced by them, yet at the same time we need space to be ourselves and to pursue our own goals unhampered by their expectations and ambitions for us.

In this context, modern relationships, as Bob and Charlotte each discovered, have an impossibly ambitious quality. Success in a relationship today is a tall order, and has come a long way from clear-cut divisions of labour and practical considerations around financial and social status. We now walk the fine line between maintaining an independent self (retain self-respect, be able to escape) and merging into a couple (embrace, compromise, submission, loss of individuality). In couples we now demand both friendship *and* eroticism, practical partnership *and* emotional support, meetings of minds *and* personal space: to be best mates and soulmates. As Adam Phillips puts it in *Monogamy,* his book of aphorisms:

The most difficult task for every couple is to get the right amount of misunderstanding. Too little and you assume you know each other. Too much, and you begin to believe there must be someone else somewhere, who does understand you. We have affairs when we get our proportions wrong.

Yet for all their fragility these loving relationships are an obvious focal point for the project of intimacy. They are the logical space in which to try the unlikely experiment of being truly connected to another. Since Plato we have been in hock to the quest for that other half. His image, from the *Symposium*, is of humans as round, eight-limbed beings sundered in two by angry gods and condemned to roam the earth looking for their unique counterpart (190–92). We are looking for the one who will finish off the sentences we begin: in our modern language of coupling, phrases such as "the other half", "Mr Right" and "you complete me" attest to this enduring ideal.

The hope for intimacy is far from the sole preserve of the romantic couple though, whether officially sanctioned partners or secret lovers with their furtive, underground projects. Friendship is another space that provides the possibility of an intimate relationship. It is to friends we turn when our romantic relationships reveal their inevitable limits. From *Butch Cassidy and the Sundance Kid* to *Thelma and Louise*, the buddy movie has traded on the notion of an exclusive, intimate bond that connects two people against the world. And as it is with friends, so it can be with family: a daughter who talks over her life choices and fears with her father or inseparable siblings who are involved in each others' lives and never let a day go by without communicating perhaps experience that special connection.

These are the kinds of relationship that traditionally promise intimacy: deep, long-lasting bonds with kith and kin. But, for various reasons I shall come to, the search for connection within those relationships is too often a fruitless one. In fact, since nearly half of Western marriages end in divorce, and many of those that survive will inevitably do so with practicalities in mind, it is reasonable to think that most relationships fail to meet the description "intimate". This is not to say that they thereby always fail as relationships. In *Howards End* (the book E. M. Forster began with that epigraph) the central couple Margaret and Henry (who we shall meet again at various points) arguably represent a worthwhile and valid relationship, but it is one that fails to be intimate. Margaret's recognition that we must "only connect" doesn't guarantee that she ever will.

The same goes for friends and family stuck in bad habits, or nostalgia, or other forms of baggage. Weighed down by too much history, constrained by a shared future, relationships are not always suitable for the baring of souls. For lurking on the other side of highly synchronized good manners can lie anger, indignation, jealousy, fear, anxiety, indifference or boredom: ultimately an enduring sense of isolation.

In contrast with relationships that aim, and often fail, to perfect a technology of intimacy (whether as partners, lovers, friends or family) are more anonymous encounters: the myriad threads that briefly link strangers, acquaintances, colleagues, even enemies. The experience of this more fleeting intimacy may be more unstable, yet for this reason it is also distilled all the more purely. The flash of recognition between strangers (eyes meeting across that proverbial crowded room, revelations on a plane journey) can be created by the very fact that the two people with their secret knowledge share neither a past nor, as yet, a future; their weightlessness, a quite bearable lightness, creates the necessary grounds for risk taking.

Intimacy is part of the everyday. It does not belong in the world of legends or heroes; rather, it sits in the small spaces that happen in everyday life, colouring the lives of those who "lived faithfully a hidden life, and rest in unvisited tombs", as George Eliot puts it. But being an everyday phenomenon does not mean we get to experience it every day. It is, in fact, maddeningly elusive for being so close at hand.

Not only is the experience vanishingly subtle, but the brutal fact is there is nothing even about the distribution of intimacy across human experience. The disparities in people's experiences of intimacy are probably at least as wide as their socioeconomic opportunities. There are so many contextual factors that create the conditions under which intimacy is even a possibility that wishing alone won't make it so. And worse than that, some people have a greater talent for intimacy than others: skills and opportunities, a secure sense of self and qualities that enable them to have more deeply satisfying encounters and make them more able to sustain relationships over time. The barriers to intimacy are not merely societal, nor are they merely interpersonal and temperamental. There is something intrinsically slippery and unsustainable about the very idea.

Fearing while desiring intimacy

Browsing for books on intimacy is revealing. First, there are so many titles that it suggests we are preoccupied with the idea. Second, many of these books focus on the difficulties inherent to this ambition. With titles like *The Intimacy Struggle*, *The Flight from Intimacy* and *Fear of Intimacy*, they convey the impression that this is difficult terrain to navigate. We are drawn to the ideal of intimacy and fear it too. Achieving it is going to require a regime and effort: it won't just come to you.

We fear our hopes for intimacy in at least two ways. The first comes from recognizing that it requires a degree of exposure or vulnerability that could be betrayed. *Fear of Intimacy*, as a typical book title, will usually be about this fear of rejection. Humiliation and shame, which lie on the other side of intimacy rebuffed, are peculiarly human kinds of pain that we will do much to avoid. The hope of connection crushed, the outstretched hand rejected, can be so hurtful it is tempting to play safe.

The second, less obvious but even more haunting, fear is that it is impossible. Listen to Samuel Beckett writing to his aunt about his love of the paintings of Jack Yeats:

> The way he puts down a man's head & a woman's head side by side, or face to face, is terrifying, two irreducible singlenesses & the impassable immensity between. I suppose that is what gives the stillness to his pictures, as though the convention were suddenly suspended … A

kind of petrified insight into one's ultimate hard irreducible organic singleness.   (Letter to Cissie Sinclair, 14 [August 1937], in Beckett 2009: 536)

"Convention" may license the claim that minds and hearts can meet – certainly this is the stock in trade of popular culture – but more uncompromising art reveals an unpalatable view, a "petrified insight" that not only do we die alone but we may live alone too.

These fears conjure up the corollary desire: a frail hope to connect despite the pain of isolation. An intimate connection is like a burning coal that can keep you warm for some time after. But we know it will not last forever. Some intimate relationships can wither (invisibly) if not fuelled by fresh intimate exchanges. One of the tragedies of old friendships is that they can come to overdepend on intimacies of the past and fail to renew and refresh their sense of each other. Relationships in general can't easily survive on past encounters; if unfuelled by new intimacies our links become attenuated.

Intimacy is finite in a literal sense too. Underlying our presentiments of mortality is the fact that grief will not last, that "time heals". The reassurance, however, has a cruel undertow. If time heals too well it does so by killing off the intimacy with the loved one, along with the need or expectation of it in the future. So while healing time is a soothing balm for grief it is a reminder that the purest intimacies will fade and die too.

But if it's all so fraught and difficult, why do we bother? Why are bookshops filled with these titles? Why does a simple parable, *Tuesdays with Morrie*, of a young man talking to his

11

dying professor and learning that the meaning of life comes down to our loving bond with others, sit on the *New York Times* bestseller list for 250 consecutive weeks, sell eleven million copies and get translated into thirty-two languages? For all its vicissitudes, the hope for intimacy lies deep in most of us. We think of ourselves as isolated individuals sometimes, but every self is socially constituted. We make no sense without our audiences, and the social animal needs others in order to live well. For human beings that feeling of being known, that shared and forgiving sense of frailty, is redemptive in a way that nothing else can be. The promise that, despite the risks or unlikelihood, we can meet E. M. Forster's injunction seems one of the most worthwhile projects to pursue in a life well lived. So we tilt at this windmill despite our fears. While Margaret struggled to achieve intimacy with Henry she didn't give up hoping:

Mature as he was, she might yet be able to help him to the building of the rainbow bridge that should connect the prose in us with the passion. Without it we are meaningless fragments, half monks, half beasts, unconnected arches that have never joined into a man. With it love is born, and alights on the highest curve, glowing against the gray, sober against the fire.

Whether in a single conversation or in a relationship built over time, intimacy can offer safety, trust and the feeling of being uniquely understood: the opposite of isolation. The possibility of intimacy is always there, if elusive. Even a brief connection made can console and comfort for some time after it has passed. By the same token, the hope for a future intimate episode, and quiet moment of mutual knowledge and acceptance, can make a relationship worth living in.

My aim in this book is to shed some light on this haunting and ubiquitous feature of human life: ubiquitous because "no man is an island, entire of itself" and haunting because of its unbearable frailty.

I shall take a closer look at varying types of intimate connection, whether between lovers, between friends or family members, between strangers or even between enemies. Along the way I shall explore the complexities and subtleties of finding intimacy as well as the barriers that impede our hopes.

2

Translating Intimacy

Intimacy, as we have seen with Bob and Charlotte, is closely tied to subtlety. John Ruskin, writing in the context of art, speaks of the small but highly significant details in paintings: "that the *minutest* portion of a great composition is helpful to the whole" calling this "the task of the least" (1869: ch. 2, esp. §1). I experienced something analogous to this on a brief trip to Venice. In the daytime I felt I was stuck in the middle of a Canaletto painting. The vivid brilliance coming at me was hard to take in. I was awed but not moved. Yet when I was on the water taxi going home from dinner, the city entered me more subtly by circuitous routes: the slopping sound of paddle in water, the candlelight in the houses. I was more profoundly affected by an indirect approach.

This is an important feature of intimacy in general. The fragility of the bond often requires a subtlety of interaction, and often something to contrast it against and thus create that sense of conspiracy. One evening Bob and Charlotte go out into Tokyo with her friends. While singing karaoke, Bob is persuaded to sing Bryan Ferry's "More Than This" and through the hilarity we can see those slight shifts of expression – a flicker, a tightening, a half-smile – that suggest a world of melancholy and desire below the surface.

Intimacy also contains ambiguity. Bob and Charlotte become deeply attached to each other without the relationship turning overtly sexual. In his review of the film, Peter Bradshaw (2004) captures the ambivalently drawn and subtle interplay well.

> Bob and Charlotte's big adventure reaches a lovely scene when they confess their most personal fears to each other, while lying on a bed, their hands not touching, their lips not meeting. It's hardly without sexual tension, but the intimacy goes beyond regular-issue desire, and when Bob tells her how he felt when his children were born, their relationship for a moment slips through the net of classification. Are they lovers? Friends? Mentor and pupil in the mysteries of life? Father and daughter?

Intimacy is not only subtle and ambiguous, but also short-lived. What is poignant about the quietness of their intimacy is how it depends on the absence of the very things we tend to cherish in our everyday relationships, to do with shared projects created over time and a sense of permanence. In contrast, their connection was enhanced by being unencumbered and by being shadowed throughout with the constant sense of an ending. The message from *Lost in Translation* is that we can only have intimacy in small doses.

At the end of his trip, when Bob leaves Charlotte and Tokyo, we are left with the burden of a connection left unexplored, as sad as it was inevitable. Then, to further meet cinematic convention at least halfway, on his way to the airport Bob improbably sees Charlotte in a crowded street, stops his cab, gets out and runs to her. They talk and then he whispers something left deliberately indistinguishable into her ear, but leaving her with a beaming smile. Does he declare love? Does he promise to meet her again? Coppola leaves this unexplained but, despite this feel-slightly-better (if not quite a feel-good) ending, we do have a sense that if they did pick up again they would also join the world of arguments and carpet samples. Their intimacy was always going to be short-lived. Equally, we have no reason to think this transformative experience will do anything to help them find intimacy with their spouses back at home.

But what is this elusive and paradoxical experience called intimacy? If we are going to look for it and avoid a simulation – such as endured by those couples locked in a grisly face-off at the local French bistro every 14 February – how can we know what to look for?

What is intimacy?

Academic articles that engage with this theme (and there are many, believe it or not) often begin with an observation that

17

while people long for intimacy, few can say what they mean by it. Read on in those articles and it quickly becomes clear that the academics also struggle to shed light on this murky concept. They sound like Augustine trying to explain the concept of time. When nobody asks me about it I know what it is. But whenever somebody asks me, I realize I don't know. Intimacy evaporates under the scholarly eye.

> One problem most central to advancing our psychological understanding of the experience of intimacy has been in defining or circumscribing the phenomenon itself. While much has been written on the topic of intimacy in a variety of contexts by both academic and "popular" authors, paradoxically, there exists less research (and even less concurrence) on … the definition of intimacy.
> (Register & Henley 1992: 467)

So claim Lisa Register and Tracy Henley in a scholarly piece on the phenomenology of intimacy. They go on to explore this diversity of approaches, identifying "at least twenty significantly different definitions of intimacy" and comment that when researchers try to analyse the topic "it is not at all clear that we are measuring or modeling the same phenomenon across differing definitions" (*ibid*.: 468).

Examples of such scholarly bafflement are legion in the academic literature. It is hardly surprising that this should be so since "intimacy" is an elusive idea with many voices. In their conclusion to the authoritative *Handbook of Closeness and Intimacy*, the editors comment that:

Ordinary people (at least in Western cultures) do seem to hold a common prototype of what creates intimacy and we can recognise common themes in researchers' definitions that are not unlike laypersons' understandings. Yet, we do not by any means have a common definition.   (Mashek & Aron 2004: 417)

If we switch from the scholarly world to dictionary definitions, the *Oxford English Dictionary* offers five for "intimacy", ten for "intimate" as an adjective (e.g. intimate knowledge), two for "intimate" as a noun (i.e. a confidant) and five more for the verb variant (such as to communicate either publicly or indirectly). These definitions overlap without really converging on a clear and easily expressible idea. They contain references to closeness and familiarity (to people or things or knowledge), to depth or intrinsic essences (e.g. "the true and intimate Substance of the Earth"), to close connections between things (e.g. "grit made up from an intimate connection of white quartz and pink felspar"). Intimate can range from describing a theatrical performance to women's underwear and, of course, is a coy euphemism for sex. Much of the usage cited in the *OED* seems more suited to historical contexts, some of it obsolete, with most of the examples drawn from the seventeenth century, when "intimacy" first came into common usage.

For a more contemporary flavour, *Merriam-Webster's Collegiate Dictionary* offers us:

intimacy ... **1**: The state of being intimate: FAMILIAR-
   ITY **2**: something of a personal or private nature

19

> **intimate** ... **1 a**: INTRINSIC, ESSENTIAL **b**: belonging to or characterizing one's deepest nature **2**: marked by very close association, contact, or familiarity [intimate knowledge of the law] **3 a**: marked by a warm friendship developing through long association [intimate friends] **b**: suggesting informal warmth or privacy [intimate clubs] **4**: of a very personal or private nature [intimate secrets]

In addition, many dictionaries repeat the line "the absence of fences created a mysterious intimacy in which no one knew privacy" in order to convey the relevant sense of closeness.

Certainly these feel on the right lines. "Closeness", "familiarity" and "belonging" all seem relevant. "Private knowledge" is right along with the removal of it through "the absence of fences". Privacy, in fact, appears to be a hallmark of how we use the term. Yet these definitions, while approaching the many ways we talk of "intimacy", seem to bleed it dry. They lack a few features that animate our preoccupation with the idea. The flatter aspects of "closeness" or "privacy" are relevant, but fail to capture the essentially dynamic or relational aspect of intimacy; and with that they also fail to capture the difficulties inherent in its pursuit. They seem to miss out the risks and pleasures of vulnerable connection, not to mention the quiet, subtle, almost ineffable force that sits at the edge of language.

If we turn to etymology, the Latin terms *intus* and *inter* ("in the midst of" and "within") bring us a little closer in their suggestion of hidden depth. The comparative *interior* ("inner, nearer, more deeply") and the superlative *intimus* ("inmost,

most profound, most hidden and secret") start to catch that sense of depth which resonates with our intuitions. The Latin verb *intimare* means "to bring in or put" or "to publish or announce". Crucially, "intimacy" is intertwined with revelation. We see this in our contemporary verb to intimate, meaning to convey even if the announcement is somewhat veiled.

Intimacy has this elusive profundity because it appeals to the essentialism that is built into human psychology. We like to plumb the hidden depths, with minds wired to look for the imagined truth that lies underneath the surface. We hope to uncover a reliable, true essence in a world of uncertainty and confusion. The natural world only encourages us in this hope. Gold, for example, is revealed precisely by the knowledge that its atomic number is 79 (the number of protons packed into the nucleus of a gold atom). If it doesn't have an atomic number of 79 it is not gold, no matter how it glisters. And this is more significant for how we see each other than anything else. The desire for intimacy is the desire to uncover the "real you" and the "real me", so as to connect them. To hope to discover an equivalent essence in a self or a personality, as we can for what philosophers call a "natural kind", like a chemical element, is a profound temptation for us.

But when it comes to people this hope is a mirage: fool's gold if you like. Our selves do not conceal an unwavering identity expressible in a formula, any more than the meaning of life (*pace The Hitchhiker's Guide to the Galaxy*) is 42. Our innermost being is a subtle, shady and complex construct shifting across our lifetimes while providing the illusion of stability, even as we cling on to the hope of permanence and reliability.

21

Isn't this why to say to someone "you've changed" so often sounds like an accusation? The obvious fact of change is a threat to the project of connection. How many relationships have failed to adapt to the brutal but unnoticed fact of transition, playing the same game long after the goalposts have moved.

Yet the illusion is a powerful one. Our minds are designed with an intuitive psychology that cannot help but attribute this essentialist view to one another, and the promise of intimacy is the promise of being vouchsafed a glimpse of your soul while offering up mine in return; despite the fact that the full blown promise is illusory.

This is not to say that intimacy is impossible, only that it is as unstable and elusive as we are, and thus is hard to define. But the deep hope is not a vain one. The feeling of mutual recognition is available even if it is rare, and even if it means recognizing that we can also make false discoveries and converge too quickly on versions of each other that obscure more than they reveal. That we must "only connect" should be redescribed in a way that depends less on the certainties of chemistry than on a more nuanced view of the intimacies we might hope for. This book is an exploration of that hope.

The different voices of intimacy

The fact that "intimacy" has many voices is easy to see. Here are some of the ways I've seen it used in one week in the *Guardian* and *Observer* newspapers: in a review of an art show, "such attention to the smallest details – even Christ's eyelashes are made of human hair – invite intimacy"; or describing women's diaries recording "mundane and intimate observations of their daily lives"; and in an interview with the film director Michael Haneke that asks about his belief in God to which he replies, "I don't answer such questions in the same way as I wouldn't answer a question about my sexual practices: it's too intimate". Then we have the familiar associations with deep learning – "his intimate involvement with the subject lends this history an emotional appeal usually absent from a scholarly work" – and, of course, music (to which we shall return shortly) – "club nights are often like relationships: the more intimate the experience, the more profoundly they can touch your soul".

These uses of "intimate" and "intimacy" invite us to look at the particular over the general. One journalist complains, "we're sick of watching travel shows that have visitors telling you what you need to see, do, feel, eat or drink. We want a personal, intimate experience of a city". Another reviews the film *They Do Not Exist*, noting that "there is a layering of narratives: the intimacy of a little girl writing a letter on a sunlit table; the power of fighter planes taking off to a Bach soundtrack; a man remembering the little girl".

In among all those usages I found only two that focused on a relationship. We have Byron, who, in his dig at William "Turdsworth", "clearly enjoyed writing slightly outrageous things to a clergyman, but you do also get a very strong sense of the depth of friendship they had. There's a real intimacy". And then we have a description of the relationship between Raymond Carver and his editor Gordon Lish (often attributed with co-creating that spare and clear-eyed prose style): "If ... you take Carver's world as a whole – the brutality of intimacy, the unplaceability of anxiety, the mess any and all of us can make of love – you may think that Lish saw something in Carver."

The metaphorical extension of the term "intimate", as seen in some of the examples above, resonates with many connotations. These include close-up scrutiny (with perhaps a voyeuristic edge), connection, privacy, depth of knowledge, the smallest scale of daily life, heightened emotion, something personal or customized (rather than standardized), friendship and ambivalence, as well as, of course, eroticism and sexuality. These rich connotations of depth and genuineness lead us to use the term to enhance and colour many experiences and are the reason intimacy is such a mainstay of marketing literature and reviews of artistic performances.

But what is striking on reading these examples is how few can be said to be about intimacy in the sense that most preoccupies us: probably just the last two (and even those are complicated by a relationship with mockery and pain). The fraught pursuit of connection between people is only a small subset of our daily usage of the word "intimate". Most of the references are to a metaphorical extension of the term to describe places, knowledge, things, performances or mood, in each case adding a richer glow over the thing it describes; and in some ways this is a lure. It is like saying that if you have dinner in our "intimate" restaurant you might find true intimacy. When not being used as a code for sex, "intimacy" takes on a poetic tone and throws a dignified light over anything we choose to shine it on: something quiet, poignant even, but also hopeful. These hopeful pointers toward intimacy show it has pathos and promise. The pathos is to do with it being a shy if not furtive need, which can be coaxed out in the right circumstances. But what is it promising? To get under the skin of things? The end of isolation?

The antidote to isolation

The promise of deep connection is so tempting that it can be overplayed. Even if there is no essence to be uncovered by an intimate we can't help yearn for that antidote to isolation: something to salve the existential ache that nobody really knows me. The ache runs deep and is one we would do much to assuage. Chuck Noland (played by Tom Hanks) in the film *Castaway* is so demented by loneliness on his desert island that he simulates a relationship with a volleyball that has washed up in one of the Fedex packages he was transporting before his plane went down. The ball has a bloodstain from his hand, which, as it dries, begins to resemble a face and this is enough for him to start to mitigate his loneliness.

Chuck talks through his days, his thoughts and feelings with Wilson (named after the company logo on the ball) as the months and years pass by in his cave. One day he has a bad argument with Wilson and kicks him into the sea, calling him a "goddam volleyball". He panics, and when he finds him again restores the face that has obviously washed off many times before, saying, "I know you, I know you, I know you" to reaffirm the synthetic bond. The implication is that if he knows Wilson, Wilson knows him, and he is not alone. And when Chuck finally loses the ball out at sea, on his successful bid to escape the island, he is overcome with genuine grief. This anthropomorphizing skill (which we extend to anything from pets to gods) testifies to our resourcefulness when it comes to dealing with loneliness.

And the ways we can feel isolated and the things we can do to try to soothe that feeling are as complicated as we are. Ironically, the depth of our loneliness comes out most clearly when we are not alone. There is nothing more alienating than being around people who do not share your values, idiosyncratic preferences, sensibilities, appetites, hopes, anxieties or sense of humour. And these are just some of the incompatibilities one can label. Sometimes the mismatch goes beyond description and we talk of not being on the same wavelength as other people, or realizing that someone "just doesn't get you". It is sometimes better to be alone than lonely in that way. Think of Rita in the film *Educating Rita*, watching her mother's silent tears during a singalong in the local pub with family and friends. Rita resolves not to follow her mother's tragic path to isolation by instead going to university and looking for "a better song to sing".

Of the many metaphorical extensions of intimacy we see, none is more common than music. The metaphor is particularly apt because intimacy puts us "in harmony" with someone else whose inner chords reverberate in synchrony with our own. So we talk of being "in tune" with someone. John Fordham's *Guardian* music blog entry on Ronnie Scott's jazz club at its fiftieth anniversary is typical: "(Ronnie) Scott ... wouldn't tolerate noise or disrespect from audiences, and he believed that a small and intimate venue like his was the ideal environment in which to appreciate the spontaneous and conversational intimacies of jazz improvisation" (2009a). In a review of a performance by Nigel Kennedy at the club Fordham describes how "A slow, chanson-like dance had the violin and tenor sax entwined, a romantic ballad of classical symmetries (which) brought a similar intimacy with pianist" (2009b).

It is little surprise that the term is so often used in descriptions of music and musical performance. Music offers a very natural link with intimacy for a couple of reasons: first, in its connotations of emotional expression, whether subtle or overt, and second, in its evocation of the ineffable. Think of a chord played on a piano. Not only do the obvious notes create a harmonious blend, but also the true timbre of the chord depends on subtle harmonics, those barely heard echoes that resonate on other unplayed strings, set off by vibrations and hovering around the main notes that are played.

Intimacy promises a level of integration and connection that runs against the series of false notes and noise that accompanies most of our everyday lives; it promises a better song to sing. And it is precisely because of intimacy's mutability and subtle texture that it is particularly difficult to express in words (in prose at any rate) as it is for music. It is more suited for showing (in a novel or a poem) than for telling (in a scholarly article or lecture). When Frank Zappa said that "talking about music is like dancing about architecture", he may as well have been talking about intimacy. Yet this language of music, while echoing some of intimacy's features on some level, pushes the concept away rather than bringing it close. It is a way of showing what the idea might connote rather than telling us what it means.

Overextending the term

Intimacy, with those musical associations, lends a honey-coloured glow to its target. The metaphorical strength of its everyday usage can cover a bewildering array of spaces. We reach for the term to ennoble or dignify and fill with promise. The hotel or restaurant that boasts intimate nooks and atmosphere is promising to create the conditions in which that music can be heard.

Because of this elastic and flattering quality there are plenty of ways the word "intimacy" is used that stretch even peripheral usage to breaking point. The US and China have an "intimately connected" economic relationship dubbed "Chimerica" by the historian Niall Ferguson. On the campaign trail Barack Obama used to be described as having a charismatic gift for creating "public intimacy". Some claim "spiritual intimacy" with God. For all I know one can find "intimate hints" in the intricate flavours of a glass of wine. In all these cases, it seems to me, we can say a couple of key ingredients are missing, and that they show how well and easily we can overextend the term. Or, to put it another way, even if we are happy with these overextended usages, they do not amount to what people are seeking in those bestselling book titles listed in the introduction to this book. Those are about escape from isolation and the hazardous feeling of being known and knowing in return.

But even *within* the scope of our normal, hopeful usage there is ambiguity to the idea of "intimacy". We use "intimate" to describe both long-term relationships and a one-off encounter between strangers. Leaving marketing literature to one side, it is striking how easily we can create yet more illusions and simulacra. Couples falsely advertise themselves as more intimate than they are with what sociologist Erving Goffman calls "the sweet guilt of conspirators". It can be cultivated between old friends or created between acquaintances thrown together in adverse circumstances. It can exist within families, between colleagues and even strangers. It can be the potent alchemy that turns acquaintances into friends, and friends into lovers.

"Intimacy", unlike "closeness" and "familiarity", which lie flatter and more safely on the page, has a quality that reverberates and unsettles: something that lies, in Pablo Neruda's words, "between the shadow and the soul". There is a lot more packed into this capacious and subversive term than is caught in a dictionary definition. It is full of contradictions. Sometimes explicit communication is involved, at other times a more subtle, unspoken variety of interaction is required. Intimacy is inherently unstable or risky, while being essentially benevolent.

So there is something uncanny and paradoxical about intimacy. For instance, going back to Webster, the fences are not just absent but must be overcome. But this means intimacy can vanish once it is achieved, because a barrier overcome is no longer a barrier. If intimacy is intimately intertwined with secrecy then it always risks undermining itself. The French philosopher Gaston Bachelard says, "there will always be more things in a closed, than in an open, box ... All intimacy hides from view" (1994: 88).

There is ultimately a limit to how well we can define the term owing to its fuzzy nature. Words sit on a spectrum from concrete to cloudy with logical terms such as "rectangle" or "bachelor" (no more or less than an unmarried man) on the one end and big, baggy concepts such as "charisma" or "love" on the other. It is no surprise that "intimacy" is at that latter extreme, scudding along in the clouds. Wittgenstein proposed the idea of *family resemblances* to describe these cloudy concepts that share no essential properties and thereby took the pressure off always having a grip on the necessary and sufficient conditions the terms we use must have. The most famous example he gave was of the term "game". What do all games have in common? If you think of the baffling array of examples, from solitaire to ring-a-ring-a-roses to professional basketball to war games, what features can we say they share? Individual or team-based, solitary or competitive, fun or serious? It is impossible to find criteria that are tight enough to capture shared features of all games without being so loose as to include other activities (such as going for a walk, or reading a book). You can't pin down the idea except to say that we know one when we see one. They are connected by *family resemblances* that can't be reduced to any particular feature. The cloudy concept is therefore like a rope, which exists despite the fact that no individual strands run its whole length.

So "intimacy", like "game", does not have a common essence that binds every example of it together. This is a function of how language works. Better to move away from the dictionary definitions and musical or other metaphors and look for good examples. In everyday language many categories we use have more prototypical as well as more peripheral or boundary cases. The category of "bird" will more readily summon up in our minds a robin than a penguin or an ostrich. The prototypical examples of "furniture" are chairs and tables rather than grandfather clocks or pianos. When talking of the fuzzy category of "intimacy" there are many forms of human interaction that might be borderline examples, such as children playing well together or a business lunch between colleagues who are also friends, but the prototypical "good example" is the romantic kiss: the icon of intimacy.

3

The Kiss

That the kiss is the icon of intimacy is so obvious it is in danger of becoming a cliché. How many romantic films end, or at least peak, with that image? The orchestra swells, the hearts melt in one long embrace. Just as clichéd is Julia Roberts's prostitute in *Pretty Woman*, who refuses to kiss on the grounds that it is too intimate. Rodin's over-familiar sculpture depicted overleaf, like Klimt's famous painting of the same name or Doisneau's photo of that couple outside the Hotel de Ville capture this fleeting moment of connection. Something deeply private, yet shared; uninhibited while turning viewers into voyeurs.

Kissing offers to blend and blur our identities for a moment. At the centre of this fully involving embrace, with extraordinary agility and sensitivity, mouths, lips and tongues meet to enable both mutual exploration and mutual yielding. An

The Kiss (1889), Auguste Rodin (photograph © Yair Haklai CC-BY-SA [http://creativecommons.org/licenses/by-sa/3.0], via Wikimedia Commons).

intimate kiss is a wordless but heightened conversation: private, reciprocal, emotional and filled with mutual desire.

Of course, not all kisses are good ones. Given the weight of expectation and the idealizations that fill our screens and books it is likely that most are not. Whether teenage kisses bedevilled by noses, teeth and self-consciousness, or more knowing ones rendered inert by familiarity or fraught with bad faith, it may be that most kisses fail to be intimate ones. Yet when kisses fail they may tell us more about what is going on in an intimate connection than when they succeed.

Howards End offers a couple of illuminating examples. The novel is a tale of two sisters (Margaret and Helen Schlegel) who are cultivated intellectuals with very knowing, although somewhat contrasting, views on the world and other people. With a sentiment formed through their German cultural heritage, they see themselves as having a more literary and passionate sensibility than offered by those "second-rank" English virtues of "neatness, decision and obedience". Helen is the ardent believer, poetic in her outlook and the romantic foil (fool?) to Margaret's more practical stance. But this is not a straightforward contrast. Helen may be presented as the embodiment of an uncompromising idea (love conquers all) but Margaret is not straightforwardly her opposite. She is more complex and, while more realistic, deeply ambivalent in a way that reflects the tensions, in other words, the choices, that the hope for intimacy forces on us all.

When it comes to making choices, Margaret is pragmatic and takes seriously the prose of everyday necessity. While she, like her sister, may harbour more romantic hopes deeper down – it is she who insists we must "only connect", after all – these inklings do not hold sway. Forster, who shows himself through many authorial intrusions in the novel, resembles Margaret and has obvious sympathy for the prose, yet, more furtively, for the poetry too.

He describes a telling kiss for each of the sisters. Helen's happens at the beginning of the novel. She is staying the night with the Wilcox family at Howards End (their country home). The father, Henry, and elder son, Charles, are startlingly unimaginative scions of the British Empire and no-nonsense businessmen. Helen falls for the more vulnerable and quieter Paul, the younger son. One evening at a small party the circumstances are set for a stolen moment: "He had drawn her out of the house, where there was danger of surprise and light; he had led her by a path he knew ... A man in the darkness, he had whispered 'I love you' when she was desiring love."

Forster is confounded by his own creation. He lacks the words to describe "that kiss" and is almost awed and revolted at once. Here he intrudes, seemingly arguing with himself as to the merits of such an experience:

That was "how it happened", or, rather how Helen described it to her sister, using words even more unsympathetic than my own. But the poetry of that kiss, the wonder of it, the magic that there was in life for hours after it – who can describe that? It is so easy for an Englishman to sneer at these chance collisions of human beings. To the insular cynic and the insular moralist they offer an equal opportunity. It is so easy to talk of "passing emotion" and to forget how vivid the emotion was ere it passed. Our impulse to sneer, to forget, is at root a good one. We recognize that emotion is not enough, and that men and women are personalities capable of sustained relationships, not more opportunities for electrical discharge. Yet we rate the impulse too highly. We do not admit that by collisions of this trivial sort the doors of heaven may be shaken open. To Helen, at all events, her life was to bring nothing more intense than the embrace of this boy who played no part in it.

In this barely coherent set of reflections, Forster is struggling to recognize the wisdom of forsaking intimacy while needing to admit its force. Plenty of critics have since found in Forster an inability to reconcile a homosexuality unacknowledged in his lifetime with his Edwardian sensibilities, and maybe this is relevant. He oscillates between "an impulse to sneer" and something else that stirs in us all if we choose to acknowledge it. And maybe there is self-knowing envy even in the "insular moralist" whose sneer is salted with awkward knowledge that, in a good life, it is right sometimes to shake open the doors of heaven.

Sadly for Helen and Paul, "that kiss" had all the vulnerability of an intimacy that cannot be sustained. By the next morning the moment has passed. Paul is cowed by the older (wiser?) men in his family and withdraws while Helen is left to recover her composure and keep the secret. The moment marks her life deeply but leaves her undeviating from her course, "because personal relations are the important thing for ever and ever, and not this outer life of telegrams and anger".

"That's foolish", replies Margaret:

> in the first place, I disagree about the outer life. Well, we've often argued that. The real point is that there is the widest gulf between my love-making and yours. Yours – was romance; mine will be prose. I'm not running it down – a very good kind of prose, but well considered, well thought out.

Margaret, by unromantic contrast, sees the concrete particulars and finds in herself "an honest English vein" that Helen detests.

> The truth is that there is a great outer life that you and I have never touched – a life in which telegrams and anger count. Personal relationships, that we think supreme, are not supreme there. There love means marriage settlements; death, death duties. So far I'm clear. But here's my difficulty. This outer life, though obviously horrid, often seems the real one – there's grit in it. It does breed character.

And her kiss, when it comes, is of this more gritty, character-building variety: somewhat horrid too. It is with Paul's father, Henry Wilcox, who she decides, to her sister's horror, to marry and thereby almost gives up on the hope of poetry. Some time after their engagement, having had no physical contact before,

Wilcox suddenly embraces her. Margaret "was startled and nearly screamed", and while she tries to kiss "with genuine love the lips that were pressed against her own" she feels afterwards that "on looking back, the incident displeased her. It was so isolated. Nothing in their previous conversation had heralded it, and worse still, no tenderness had ensued … he had hurried away as if ashamed".

A shot at intimacy that misses its target will easily carry an undertow of shame. Margaret continues to make a life with Henry, for what it's worth. And for her it is worth a great deal. In any case, she has the measure of Wilcox and knows what she is getting into. Is she lying back and/or thinking of England? She sees that he is afraid of emotion and cares too much about success, and his sympathy "lacks poetry, and so isn't sympathy really". She knows he will never know her well and yet cannot give up entirely on the hope for intimacy with him.

> She would only point out the salvation that was latent in his own soul, and in the soul of every man. **Only connect!** That was her whole sermon. Only connect the prose and the passion, and both will be exalted, and human love will be seen at its height. Live in fragments no longer. Only connect, and the beast and the monk, robbed of the isolation that is life to either, will die.

The connection that she and Forster are pursuing hopes to cut across both the external barriers of class and context and the internal tensions of *eros* and *pragma*. It combines the

39

liberal hope of solidarity with a more idiosyncratic dream of fused personalities: a wholesale search for integration through intimacy with others. Is this ambition to connect the prose and the poetry, to do justice to both, too ambitious? Are we condemned to a life in fragments? In so far as her relationship with Henry Wilcox is concerned, the sad answer for Margaret is yes. While she commits to loving him, intimacy is never within reach.

Looking at kisses can tell us something about what intimacy means even if, as I've said, we see this most clearly in the failed ones. And so Margaret's kiss tells us more than Helen's. First, it crucially lacks a reciprocal element. She was taken by surprise and, unlike the movie cliché, there were no violins; she did not respond to his manhandling. It also lacks the kind of emotion and insight from the hemmed in Mr Wilcox that true intimacy requires.

But there is more to intimacy than the expression of emotion, insight and mutual desire that was missing from this last example. There is something darker, conspiratorial or at least more poignant in the truly prototypical example: the shared secrecy of private revelation. If we return to Rodin there is a little more to see in that sculpture that helps it to be such a good exemplar. This particular kiss, sculpted in 1886, is not a straightforward one. It represents Francesca da Rimini, the thirteenth-century Italian noblewoman immortalized in Dante's *Inferno*, after having fallen in love with her husband's younger brother Paolo Malatesta. *The Kiss* represents their fleeting and vulnerable intimacy, soon to be cut short when they are later discovered and killed by Francesca's jealous husband, Giovanni. Doesn't the image become all the more intimate for knowing that it is a *secret and hazardous* kiss?

By contrast, if we imagine Paolo feeling crowded out by Francesca, perhaps ashamed and guilty about his brother to the point where his mind has wandered, the intimacy surely drains away. Intimacy is a spectrum; it is not a binary concept that is on or off. It grows or shrinks under different conditions. The Rodin *Kiss* shows its elasticity by becoming more central or more peripheral an example of intimacy depending on the situation.

Given the significance of context, the poignancy of intimacy can be created in many settings, and while many (if not most) kisses are lacking in some ingredient or other, other less intimate-seeming examples of interaction between people can take on this quality in a second, as long as they have some key features in place.

PART ONE

Intimacy Through Four Lenses

The intimacy I believe we crave comes from that feeling of true connection, a mutual recognition that Margaret Schlegel analysed and understood even if she didn't find it with Henry (and which Helen aimed for more uncompromisingly but ultimately fruitlessly): what she called "the rainbow bridge that should connect the prose in us with the passion. Without it we are meaningless fragments, half monks, half beasts, unconnected arches".

We crave it because it promises to fulfil a deep need we have for being known and knowing in return. The social animal cannot live well in fragments with the thought of being as "irreducibly single" as Samuel Beckett described. We are connectors. Because the need we have runs so deep, we know we are vulnerable to disappointment; either because we shall never find a genuine connection, or because we shall fall for an illusion and get hurt. Often it feels better not to look for it in the first place than to try and fail. We may want to know and feel known in return, but the recognition must be of a certain kind. It must be genuine, benevolent and trusting. The undertow of intimacy unfulfilled is shame and humiliation.

But our disappointments do not stop there, for even when we achieve this type of connection with someone we know it is intrinsically short-lived, and must fade. Intimate moments cannot be trusted to endure.

While the academic literature is not clear-cut in its conclusions about intimacy, there does seem to be some convergence, some key lenses at least through which to look at the experience. In their contribution to the *Handbook of Personal Relationships*, Harry Reis and Philip Shaver (1988) have proposed an influential model. Their claim is that intimacy requires something more than reciprocity and disclosure, but an interaction that is validating and accepting of the one who discloses.

To lay out my cards it seems to me that the clearest examples of intimacy have the following four characteristics: they are *reciprocal*, *conspiratorial*, *emotional* and *kind*. Margaret Schlegel's rainbow bridge that keeps us from being mere unconnected arches has light refracted through these four lenses. The features interlink and blend but help, it seems to me, to describe the family resemblances that exist during intimate experiences. The metaphor of refracted light also helps to show the frailty of intimacy too. Light and illusion go together and, knowing this, we, like Nabokov's fictional poet

John Shade's waxwing, might easily be "slain/ by the false azure in the window pane".

Each of these lenses has attributes that enable intimacy. The reciprocal one offers mutual recognition: a simultaneous knowingness or awareness of each other. Something about acknowledgement (often unstated), about seeing and being seen, is crucial to the experience. The conspiratorial element indicates that this awareness must be to some degree concealed from people outside that intimate connection, and this secret sharing brings with it vulnerability (to exposure or betrayal) and the need for trust (which links to the fourth feature of kindness). The third characteristic of intimacy is that it is emotionally heightened. This is important for two reasons. The first and more obvious comes from a feeling of significance that comes with heightened emotion. Our emotions are the indicator that something actually matters to us and concentrate our attention accordingly. The second reason is that emotions are to some extent outside our control and not easily deployed for mere tactical reasons.

Both the second and third (the conspiratorial and the emotional) lenses threaten our reputations somewhat. We put a lot of energy into coming across as nice and in control: the twin peaks of a good reputation. Since no one is as nice or as in control as they would like to seem, the knowledge we seek of them needs to be confident of getting past the PR. With the second and third features, secrets and emotions, we are left exposed to the judgement of others. The first can easily threaten your chance of appearing nice and the second the chance of appearing in control.

45

Intimacy requires a leap of faith because it involves recognition of the hazardous fact that others might know you better than you know yourself. Knowing yourself is out of reach owing to the self-deceptive tendencies of maintaining a good reputation. That's why all the kids in Lake Woebegone are above average. In *Being and Nothingness*, Sartre once observed that character only exists in so far as it becomes an object of knowledge in the eye of another. "Consciousness does not know its own character – unless in determining itself reflectively from the standpoint of another's point of view" (2003: 372). He is saying, in effect, that when I look out at the world I am necessarily looking away from myself and, even as I try to catch glimpses, my self "is like a shadow which is projected on a moving and unpredictable material" (*ibid.*: 285–6).

To allow someone else to know us in ways we cannot know ourselves is to renounce the need to control impressions and open up the space for others to see us as they might wish. What they see won't be the whole truth either, but it might, if accurate enough and well motivated enough, navigate the hazardous path to a greater intimacy. And this is where the fourth characteristic comes in. We hope for that judgement to be kind. "Intimacy", at heart, requires a benevolent stance towards the other person based on trust, respect or affection: a willingness to think well of each other despite having the tools at our disposal to undermine or to be cruel.

It is quite rare for human interaction to have all of these present in high degree, but common enough to experience some combination of them to some degree. Friendly chats with strangers, group-bonding, difficult conversations and nostalgic reverie all might come close but often lack one or more of these elements. We have pleasant enough encounters that meet many of the safe near-definitions of closeness of familiarity but that lack a certain something – the emotion tone, the confidences exchanged, the mutual engagement, the "darkness visible" – leaving one feeling that the experience in question, although pleasurable and valuable, was not a very intimate one.

Here is an extreme example to make the point. A cruel person can provide light shone painfully through the first three lenses, but without kindness it feels more like a burning searchlight. Witness the curious near intimacy of O'Brien toying with Winston Smith in *1984*:

> Do you remember writing in your diary that it did not matter whether I was a friend or enemy, since I was at least a person who understood you and could be talked to? You were right. I enjoy talking to you. Your mind appeals to me. It resembles my own mind except that you happen to be insane.

Take kindness away from intimacy and you get torture.

Intimacy doesn't have to look like Rodin's *Kiss* – in fact, the sexual connotation is something of a distraction because most intimate moments are not sexual, and plenty of sexual moments are not intimate – but it does have to have a quality of special connection. With these four lenses in place that connection, it seems to me, is focused on that seemingly direct availability of one to the other, which we call intimacy.

Each of these features provides a different lens through which to explore the vagaries and vicissitudes of the human desire to connect. Each has its internal dynamic and its challenges. Each of them has conditions that make them more or less possible, each of them is enabled and constrained by the language we use or avoid, and the culture we inhabit. And intimacy, as I've said, is not all or nothing. The light can be focused or blurry. It seems to me, however, that the strong presence of all four of these characteristics is the hallmark of intimacy at its most clear and distinct. As any or all of them fade or blur, so the experience starts to shade into something else. And since these characteristics are complex and mutable, I shall look at each of them in more detail.

4

~

It Takes Two

One of the reasons intimacy and love are not the same thing (although clearly they share some features) is the fact that intimacy is intrinsically reciprocal. It is not a trait or a state. Love, like other emotional states, can be seen as characteristic of an individual, while intimacy is of necessity a relational idea, like conversation. Love fundamentally is a different thing because you can love someone who doesn't love you back and you can also love an idealized or distorted version of the person. This is where love is more like infatuation. For intimacy we need more accurate knowledge of each other and mutuality. Ultimately, unlike love, hate or any other emotion, intimacy exists *between* rather than within people; you can experience unrequited love, but you cannot experience unrequited intimacy.

Intimacy is often confused with, or subsumed within, love because we associate the strength of feeling and the vulnerability that can be true of both as meaning they are parts of the same experience. Yet we can have love without intimacy and intimacy without love. Lovers can often experience intimacy, of course, but so can friends and even strangers. Equally, lovers can be baffled by a lack of connection.

The need for a reciprocal element to intimacy leads to some controversial claims. As we saw earlier, we often use the term in ways that overextend it, such as saying someone has intimate knowledge of her subject. The word will serve well enough in that context but the intimacy we crave in general needs a knowing partner. Mutual knowledge is a technical concept in logic. It contrasts with individual knowledge, where I know something and you know something. Mutual knowledge takes a crucial additional step: I know that you know that I know.

Intimacy requires this flash of mutual recognition, this knowingness, which means both parties are awake and aware of what is passing between them. So if "intimacy" depends on this mutual awareness, then, I would argue that a mother kissing her sleeping child is not intimate, even if we often describe it as such in our everyday extension of the term. This is because the child is unaware and the closeness is one-sided. The same goes for the nurse carefully and respectfully closing the eyes of a patient who has just died, or Tom Hanks's companionship with his volleyball, Wilson, in *Castaway*: tender, yes, poignant and emotional, of course, but one-sided and therefore not intimate.

What these other scenes lack, however moving, is the feeling of knowing and being known in return: in short, mutual recognition. The near awareness in this description by Julian Barnes from his *A History of the World in 10½ Chapters* comes very close but I'd argue falls short:

> Anyway ... she's asleep, turned away from me on her side. The usual stratagems and repositionings have failed to induce narcosis in me, so I decide to settle myself against the soft zigzag of her body. As I move and start to nestle my shin against a calf whose muscles are loosened by sleep, she senses what I'm doing, and without waking reaches up with her left hand and pulls the hair off her shoulders on to the top of her head, leaving me her bare nape to nestle in. Each time she does this I feel a shudder of love at the exactness of this sleeping courtesy.

This is a borderline case because "she senses what I'm doing" but it is not a truly intimate connection in the sense I am trying to explore, again due to that lack of mutual knowledge.

By contrast, another borderline example that I would see as intimate, even though it involves a very young child possibly at the earliest stage of being able to reciprocate, comes from a woman reporting an experience to a researcher studying intimacy:

> The intimate moment I would like to describe happened in December 1985. A friend of mine had a premature baby who remained hospitalized for 6 months. When

the baby arrived home from the hospital, it was to a very depressed mother, who had just buried another child. She could not relate to the baby and he was not thriving ... 9 months old and only 7 pounds, very irritable, and very sick. His prognosis at the time was not good. People were afraid of him and afraid to touch him. When my friend was hospitalized with severe depression she had no one to care for him and I volunteered. I was very nervous when I approached the little fellow. He looked like nothing more than a shriveled up little old man, with very wise and sad eyes. His mom had never held him. I went over to where he was lying and sat down and started just looking at him. I have this thing I do with babies: I sit very quietly and from inside myself I start feeling love and warmth. I just sit and let the feelings wash over me and then when I'm sure all the feelings are at a high level, I look directly into the child's eyes. I don't say anything or smile or gesture. I simply try to communicate peace and warmth and love. I did that with this little one. He started changing before my eyes. At first he just looked and then he caught my eyes with his. That direct eye contact was the key to something inside him. Maybe he felt my lack of fear and love at the moment. He became a little boy and smiled and reached for me. When I picked him up and hugged him to myself, it was one of those rare moments in my life that I have been truly and completely happy. He bonded to me at that moment and I was always there for him. I became his "mommy" for 7 months and I hope we'll always be friends.   (Register & Henley 1992: 477)

The key here is that reciprocal element: the mutuality of the experience. By contrast, confidences revealed in the doctor's office, or to lawyers and therapists are held off from intimacy by professional conventions restricting too much "involvement". For this reason these conversations are not in themselves intimate even though we speak of intimate revelations. Intimacy might begin, by contrast, just at the moment that professional boundaries are crossed.

For related reasons, intimacy is exclusive. By this I mean it exists between two people and thereby to some extent excludes others. This is another controversial aspect of my claim because it leads to the conclusion that intimacy does not really exist in groups. A sports team winning a game, a group at work winning a tender, can find a moment of intense belonging or affection. These, it seems to me, are examples of communality, a strongly shared sense of community, rather than intimacy.

The suggested counter-examples I've heard are of this type: a group of young men are on holiday together. They routinely stay up late, drinking heavily, wake up with hangovers and meet for brunch on the beach. And on one of those occasions, as they are talking and eating, a moment of awareness descends on them. They go quiet and feel all of a sudden that nothing more needs to be said to underline their closeness. Another is the moment when singers in a choir suddenly reach a moment of mutual understanding and begin a crescendo together without instruction from a conductor. Or think of a convivial dinner party, laughing, drinking and breaking bread.

Again, one can see the attraction of calling these intimate moments. So why do I feel they do not quite fit the bill? The sociologist Georg Simmel has some insight on this question: "Now there is the matter of how the intimate character of the dyadic bond is connected to its sociological specificity, forming from it no higher unity over its individual elements" ([1908] 1992: 86).

What I take Simmel to be saying is that there is something special about a twosome that is quite different from a group. The "dyad" exists in a way where each person is fully accountable to the other. By contrast, where a group is formed, even by merely adding a third person, a somewhat different dynamic comes into play. There is now a group identity and structure, a "higher unity", that is somehow above and beyond the people themselves: a club in which they are now all members and through which the whole becomes greater than the sum of its parts. That superstructure starts to shape the relationships within it. As he goes on to say: "The more extensive a community is the easier it is, on the one hand, for an objective unity to form over the individuals, and, on the other, the less intimate it becomes" (*ibid.*). This is not true for a dyad where there is nothing other than the two people involved who bear full responsibility for the part they play in the pair.

The gaze

Apart from language, vision is the key route through which we apprise ourselves of each other's minds. It is the way we pay attention. So much of our relations with each other depend on exquisite control of our gaze; in knowing when to offer it or when to withdraw it. Because of the sheer uncanny significance of eye contact, it is hard to sustain and can quickly become unbearable. In fact there are very few occasions where sustained eye contact is apt: the intimacy is too intense much of the time. For similar reasons the politeness of strangers in everyday life depends on the suitable averting of one's gaze.

As Goffman puts it in *The Presentation of Self in Everyday Life*, "in a public place, one is supposed to keep one's nose out of other people's activity and go about one's business" (1990: 224). He calls the half-acknowledgements we give to each other in urban settings "civil inattention". The point being that this ordered shape of public life doesn't just happen automatically: it is "done" or "achieved" by us in myriad ways, including by suitably averting our gaze. By contrast, one of the pleasures of cinema is that we can look closely into someone's eyes without fear of rebuke. In real life, only the mad and the besotted stare into the eyes of strangers for too long.

There is something in the gaze that singles out its object, and becomes the object of the other's gaze in return. We cannot fully attend to more than one thing at a time, as anyone who has tried to have a conversation in person while listening to someone else on the phone will attest. This is one of the reasons we find intimacy in shorter supply in a digital age of multitasking and simultaneous communication streams. I shall return to the question of intimacy and new media in Chapter 11.

It is a commonplace among interviewers that much of what you need to know about another person is resolved in the first few moments. We sum the interviewee up in a Gladwellian Blink. Looking at another's face goes beyond abstract analysis but is a holistic, wordless blend of perception and judgement of the other. Simmel has something to say about this too. This gestalt perception of another face is his basis for claiming that "a man is first known by his countenance, not by his acts" ([1908] 1921: 359). He goes on to say that this "initial impression" "remains ever the keynote of all later knowledge of him; it is the direct perception of his individuality which his appearance, and especially his face, discloses to our glance" (*ibid.*: 360). In jumping to conclusions we may well make mistakes, but we seem to jump nevertheless.

Looking someone in the eye is as direct a promise of intimacy (or anger) as there can be. In comprehending someone this way we learn who we are dealing with and what to expect from them. Isn't this why eyes are called windows to the soul? As Simmel goes on to comment: "By the glance which reveals the other, one discloses himself. By the same act in which the observer seeks to know the observed, he surrenders himself to be understood by the observed" (1969: 358). This creates grounds for intimacy in which it is hard to maintain one's reserve and requires a high degree of trust and as a joint act of self-surrender is, for Simmel, "the most perfect reciprocity in the entire field of human relations" (*ibid.*).

Of course it's not so simple. The cinematic trope may have eyes reliably meeting across that crowded room, but in reality we are less omniscient. Interviews are notoriously unreliable ways to hire people. While we have a gift for recognizing faces and interpreting facial expression, the attempt to fathom another person in this way is challenging and often disquieting. When it comes to capturing another person through language we are forced to commit to an account at least: a description that may simplify but at least creates a sense of a person with whom we can do business, as it were. By contrast the wordless, holistic, mutual glance is filled with a puzzling ambiguity: apparently deeper, yes, but inchoate as a Rembrandt self-portrait.

So the mutual gaze or glance enables intimacy on one level but takes it away on another. It offers that holistic insight into the other while yielding up the self in return; it also potentially confounds because of the sheer complexity of the task. In looking into another's face we both know and don't know. Whether they are windows on to the soul or "false azure", eyes reveal and conceal with equal alacrity. And where we fear they may reveal too much we have reason to mask or disguise our facial expressions entirely (liars often avoid eye contact entirely) making the interpretive task harder. So for various reasons our interpretation is more than likely to fall short.

And when intimacy misses its mark the possibility of shame arises, which will also incline one to look away, just in case. Sometimes the safer path is a furtive glance, which sits between a gesture towards connection and a simultaneous shying away so as to escape rejection. But the safe path comes at a price; in avoiding too candid a look, intimacy can be avoided too.

Without reciprocity, eye contact denied achieves the opposite of intimacy. Prisoners waiting for execution are often hooded or blindfolded so as to be reducible to a less potent witness for those who have dehumanizing work to do. We close the eyes of the dead as if to recognize that to look for that mutual glance with them is illusory.

And all-seeing but one-way supervision can create the conditions in which intimacy is impossible. Sartre would say our unease at being stared at comes from the dread that we are being reduced to a mere object by "the eye of the other". Medusa's gaze turned people to stone.

Insight without intimacy

In George Orwell's dystopian novel *1984*, we see what life looks like when genuine connection seems out of reach. In a world where Big Brother is always watching it is impossible to cultivate the conspiratorial exclusivity that is the hallmark of intimacy. The telescreen in every room works like Jeremy Bentham's Panopticon: the ideal glass prison in which the guards were in the centre, keeping the prisoners under constant, inescapable supervision. If you "remained within the field of vision which the metal plaque commanded", you "could be seen as well as heard": "You had to live – did live, from habit that became instinct – in the assumption that every sound you made was overheard, and except in darkness, every movement scrutinized."

In the novel most of the population seem to be brainwashed enough not to realize what is missing, yet in their midst is the irreducibly human Winston Smith. Our everyman in a world of zombies, Winston shows our cravings to ourselves. He represents the need to get past the general slab of moral will to a truer connection. He finds this in Julia, his lover, but, more interestingly, as we saw earlier, he also looks for this in his torturer, O'Brien. When Winston wrote in his diary that "everything follows" from the freedom to say that two plus two equals four, it was not an entirely privatized thought. As Orwell comments, he had "the feeling he was speaking to O'Brien". Winston describes himself as "writing the diary for O'Brien – to O'Brien"; it was like a never-ending letter that no one would read, but which was addressed to a particular person and took its shape and texture from that fact.

O'Brien is able to destroy Winston by getting so close to him. This intensity of exploration – and intensely felt, one assumes, by O'Brien too – leads to Winston facing his ultimate fear of rats in Room 101 and dismantling himself with the fatally treacherous sentence "Do it to Julia!" Only by recognizing in Winston a quality of mind similar to his own and through studying him minutely over time, and by offering the promise of a reciprocal closeness in return, can O'Brien achieve a destruction so complete. One might argue it is precisely because the relationship was a nearly intimate one that Winston cannot recover or ignore its significance. Intimacy approximated carries with it the undertow of shame and humiliation. But without true reciprocity it remains an approximation.

Reasserting the self

There are shades of grey and borderline cases here. We cannot say that intimacy depends on the gaze or mutual recognition *per se*, although this can distil it into a particularly pure form. The point is only to say that prototypical examples of intimacy, the ones that meet the prescript "only connect" most successfully, are at once together and separate and aware, and fundamentally reciprocal. Separate is as important as together. What we see in some loving or dependent relationships is a submergence of the self. Couples start to talk as though they were an entity, distinct from the individuals they used to be: "We don't go to those restaurants", "We love Woody Allen". The private work of intimacy demands a reassertion of one's uniqueness, all the more so for it to be understood by the other, rather than translated into groupthink. We shall return to this in Chapter 10, "Wishful Thinking".

Returning to the group of young men on the beach, let's imagine that the night before, two of them had a drunken fumble together. If, in that moment of silence the next day, one caught the other's eye with a meaningful glance, would we not identify an intimacy between the two, within the larger group bond? And wouldn't that also be true if in the choir a soprano catches the eye of a tenor to share a quiet in-joke about the conductor? Doesn't the knowing look, the secret sharing that comes from a mischievous smile, indicate a mutuality that splits pairs of individuals off from the group as a whole?

To put it another way, the group settings I've described – the group of friends, the choir, the sports team, the work unit – are in some ways about submergence of the self to the larger group identity: Simmel's "higher unity". Each self is joined up to something greater and this can be a profoundly desirable thing. Community and solidarity can be deeply moving and satisfying. But by contrast, in the mutual recognition that comes from intimacy it seems to me that one's unique identity is preserved, not submerged, and if anything enhanced, while accepted by the eye of another knowing, sympathetic, idiosyncratic self. That kind of attention takes two.

This also means that a pair of individuals needs certain skills that are less of a priority in a group setting: the forensic skills of a detective, the imaginative skills of a novelist, the expressive skills of an actor, to name a few. I shall return to the skill we need when looking at the barriers to intimacy later in this book. In *The Ego Trick*, the philosopher Julian Baggini contrasts two views of the self: what he calls the "pearl view", which assumes that we have a hard centre, an unvarying essence (*à la* that pot of gold), that is waiting to be discovered, and the "bundle" view of the self, which was initiated by David Hume and challenges the pearl view with a recognition of the multifaceted features that better describe who we truly are. Baggini convincingly argues that the bundle view is the correct one, despite our appetite for "pearl diving". He quotes the Buddhist philosopher Stephen Batchelor as saying:

> The self in some ways, in its more neurotic aspects, as something fixed, is basically a crystallization of a certain craving, a certain grasping. It's like if you tighten your fist very very tight you will get to a point where it feels like it is a kind of solid thing, whereas in fact it's not. And as you release your grasp, the hand is still just as much there

but now it's able to do all sorts of stuff and it doesn't feel solidified in the same way.

(Baggini 2011: 233, quoting Batchelor)

The pearl view is hard to shake off, and satisfies as much it misleads. The general point to make here is that we are far more complicated than words allow and thus very hard to interpret accurately. In his book on how hard it is for a computer program ever to model the human mind, *Gödel, Escher, Bach*, Douglas Hofstadter has a brief excursus on the odd associations that can float through an ordinary head:

Driving down a country road, you run into a swarm of bees. You don't just duly take note of it; the whole situation is immediately placed in perspective by a "swarm" of replays that crowd into your mind. Typically, you think, "Sure am lucky my window wasn't open!" – or worse, the reverse: "Too bad my window wasn't closed!" "Lucky I wasn't on my bike!" "Too bad I didn't come along five seconds earlier." Strange but possible replays: "If that had been a deer, I could have been killed!" "I bet those bees would have rather had a collision with a rosebush." Even stranger replays: "Too bad those bees weren't dollar bills!" "Lucky those bees weren't made of cement!" "Too bad it wasn't just one bee instead of a swarm" "Lucky I wasn't the swarm instead of being me." (2000: 641)

I don't know how typical this particular example may be but it serves to show us the swarm of impressions that can

62

create a self, and which cycle through us for no good reason, some of them barely impinging on our consciousness. It is a typical illustration of how untypical we all are. This indicates the sheer scale of that demanding and obscure task: knowing another person.

Mutual knowledge is very difficult to achieve between two people, let alone in a larger group, and may be illusory when felt. For now let us acknowledge how hard it is for you to have a good insight into just one other person, and for that person to understand you in return. The atomic number of a soul is not available for inspection. How do I know that you know me or that I know you? How can I be vouchsafed an accurate glimpse without falling for a fiction? If I look into your face do I see what Rembrandt might have seen? If not your true golden essence, surely I can view your distinctiveness, your character, in a way that accords with your own sincerely held view of yourself. But the real you is not stable enough for me to get a sufficiently tight grip. An accurate knowledge of you is going to recognize that what once was true can quickly fade from view. And so it is for me, if I don't avert my gaze. If I look honestly enough at myself I'll see the incoherence and inconsistency: the un-narrated randomness.

It is hard enough for intimacy to demand a reciprocal understanding between two people – too hard much of the time – not least since so much of what needs to be understood is, for various reasons, concealed. This takes us to the second characteristic of intimacy.

5

A Conspiracy

What is it to know someone else? Much as intimacy demands mutual knowingness, this is a particularly difficult and paradoxical task.

> I am caught in this contradiction: on the one hand, I believe I know the other better than anyone and triumphantly assert my knowledge to the other ("*I* know you – I'm the only one who really knows you!"); and on the other hand, I am often struck by the obvious fact that the other is impenetrable, intractable, not to be found; I cannot open up the other, trace back the other's origins, solve the riddle. (Barthes 2002: 134)

Roland Barthes is writing about love in *A Lover's Discourse*, but the insight is relevant. I've made much of the fact that mutual knowledge is key to the experience of intimacy and yet, as we have seen, it is a tantalizingly elusive experience.

In a parenthetical aside Barthes pins down more precisely what this elusive knowledge consists in: "Of everyone I had known, X was certainly the most impenetrable. This was because you never knew anything about his desire: isn't *knowing someone* precisely that – knowing his desire?"

Why are we so sure that the truth lies within? Barthes' insight that to know someone is to know what they desire brings with it the relevant corollary: because not all desires lie on the surface. Or, where we find them on the surface, we feel we are encountering a lie. Is this why the feeling of discovery is so key to the experience of intimacy? It is the hallmark of a trustworthy insight. We can widen the concept from desire to motivation more generally. To know someone is to know her motives. What she cares about, or worries about, or longs for, or regrets or is moved by. Motives move us in the most literal sense. And many of those motives, like desires, are of necessity hidden.

Secret knowledge

It does not take much to acknowledge how much must be concealed from others to preserve a good reputation; and a good reputation is crucially important to the successful functioning of a social animal. No one can do without being credible. We need to be credited in two ways in particular – with being well motivated and with being competent – if we are to get by and to be trusted and liked enough to participate in the social sphere. It was the psychologist Elliot Aronson (1976) who concluded that cognitive dissonance (the discomfort triggered by the need to suppress contradictory beliefs and behaviours) arises most when we have to repair threats to our image of seeming nice or in control. Lacking the first makes you look bad, lacking the second makes you look mad. And to avoid lacking either means hiding the contradictory, embarrassing, weak-willed, grandiose or in many ways unacceptable motives we have from polite society. So secrets abound.

I say we all know how much we conceal, but even this is not so straightforward. If we thought we were feigning all the time this would eat away at the very self-image, the nice and controlled one, we so need to protect. Most of the time we feel more surefooted than that. We have evolved the remarkable capacity for self-deception that enables a self-serving but genuine sincerity. After all, some of the best liars have convinced themselves first. We may catch a glimpse in our dreams, or in our overreactions to things, that there is more going on, but most of the time the lid is firmly on.

Motives are hard to pin down because they spring from sources we cannot easily fathom, they are unruly and self-contradictory and rely on wilful blindness if our egos are going to achieve anything like mastery in their own houses. I have described these aspects of hidden, contradictory motives in my book *Deception*.

What does it say for the secret sharing that is necessary for intimacy if I am not aware of my own secrets? If intimacy requires knowing other peoples' motives and revealing our own to others we can sense the impediments to connection here. What we want so often clashes up against obstacles, convention, rules and what others want (for you or for themselves). We don't want to feel exposed and most of the time we hide. Our everyday is a rhythm of fluent activity and coordination. Whether working or playing, the routines and habits guide us away from our rich interiority. We distort what we want so that it fits convention and so there is no danger. Our public language of desires enables a hearty convergence that smoothes over the subtle timbre of our motives. In the process the possibility of genuine connection is undermined.

In the film *Educating Rita*, Rita goes to university in pursuit of that better song to sing. She makes new friends and in particular is wowed by the apparently bohemian and confident Trish (played by Maureen Lipman). "Wouldn't you just die without Mahler?" is Trish's refrain, soon to be adopted, with naive enthusiasm, by Rita, who changes her accent on Trish's advice because "there is not a lot of point in discussing beautiful literature in an ugly voice". They become "best friends" by keeping the intimacy of true knowledge at bay.

Self-deception is, by definition, hard to spot in oneself. If you could it wouldn't be working very well. But for my purposes it is enough to see how well we can spot it in others. Rita may need Trish's attempted suicide to help the scales fall from her eyes, but we, in the knowing audience, can see the false consciousness from the beginning. We know that Rita has been suckered by the bohemian play-acting and can see how self-deludingly sincere she is as she explains all to her disappointed teacher, Frank. As he puts it: "Found a better song to sing, have you? No – you have found a different song, that's all. And on your lips it's shrill and hollow and tuneless."

This knowingness we share with Frank means we do not easily trust those surface desires. We can't help the awkward insight that only very young children can be said to be unencumbered selves. Their expressed desires are to be trusted, but this is not so for adults. We all sing our different songs and we instinctively see them as so much PR and advertising to help others traffic effectively in the social world. We know that others at least clothe their motives and desires as carefully as they clothe their bodies – "I'm just a regular guy", "I'm not racist, but ...", "Wouldn't you just die without Mahler?" – with all the taste and discretion that goes into achieving a particular style (whether affectedly manicured or nonchalantly unkempt).

The need for discovery

It is clear that disclosure is important for the experience of intimacy. The etymology reminds us of this. To feel we have come to know someone, and to feel known in return, we must peer past the smoke to glimpse the fire within. Nothing less will do. This is why intimacy is a conspiracy and it is one of the reasons people feel jealous or uncomfortable when they see others who have managed that bond, who have that private chemistry. Witnessing an in-joke, or a whispered comment, or a knowing look from the outside is hard to ignore, as is being ignored.

Revelations are often deep, but even a trivial example can quickly create the conditions for intimacy as long as a secret is being shared. One way to see how this might work is to look at a borderline case. If I'm standing at the bar it's fairly obvious that I want to buy a drink. When the man behind the bar catches my eye to acknowledge me, is that intimate? No. A gaze met is not sufficient. If I step into a revolving door and I see someone else do the same through the glass it's not hard for us to coordinate our motives. I want to get into the building and she wants to get out. We coordinate our pushing; we exchange a look. But is that intimate? Again no, for the same reason: because nothing has been uncovered. But what if instead the man behind the bar is angered by his colleague blocking his access to the till and he looks up at the ceiling in exasperation, mouths an expletive, and then looks back at me to see if I've noticed. I have, and now this more charged look we exchange, behind the other barman's back, as it were, can be a somewhat intimate one.

In truth, how much more do I know about the barman than before? Not much. The only difference between those two looks is the sense of revelation. The gaze is all the more potent for being hidden from onlookers.

The psychoanalyst Erich Fromm comments in *The Art of Loving* that:

The basic need to fuse with another person so as to transcend the prison of one's separateness is closely related to another specifically human desire, that to know the "secret of man". While life in its merely biological aspects is a miracle and a secret, man in his human aspects is an unfathomable secret to himself – and to his fellow man … The further we reach into the depth of our being, or someone else's being, the more the goal of knowledge eludes us. Yet we cannot help desiring to penetrate into the secret of man's soul, into the innermost nucleus …

(2000: 27)

As implied, we should be careful here. The consequence of our distrusting eye being unable to take surface motives at face value is that we can't help give the uncovered one more credence (whether it deserves it or not). Disclosure and discovery are the hallmark of apparent truth. "Aha! *In vino veritas*", we say as the covers of sobriety are lifted. This goes back to the search for buried treasure I discussed earlier: that need to uncover the essential, golden essence, however mythical, of a true self underneath the distracting exterior.

We can see the mechanism working even in the borderline example in the bar. How much more intense an invitation to intimacy comes from the melodrama of a more wrenching admission? In the film *Dangerous Liaisons* there is a scene where the Vicomte de Valmont (played by John Malkovich) is attempting to seduce Madame de Tourvel (Michelle Pfeiffer) as they spend time together at a country estate. Over a period of weeks Valmont tries comically and ineffectually to pique her interest, and then to convince her that he loves her and is willing to reform. He desperately looks to counter his reputation as a Don Juan and, through acts of staged piety, manages to cause her to rethink her disdain for him. Nevertheless, even

as enmity turns to friendship, she seems immune throughout. She has been resisting his charms for weeks and then
one night when she is ill he comes to her and manages to
overpower her. Up until that point her self-image was that
of a completely virtuous woman. She would not even have
recognized her underlying attraction to Valmont had someone accused her of it. And then he happened upon her at
a vulnerable time and she yielded. Her suppressed passion
now revealed overcame her and he was in a position to take
advantage. He held back. He saw something else in her – her
helplessness, her need to maintain a good reputation – and
in recognition of those more important (if less urgent) needs
he held back.

That intimate scene has all the components: mutual knowledge, a sense of discovery, heightened emotion and kindness.
But on the second feature, that sense of discovery, we can see
the quirk of psychology that insists the revealed motive is the
deeper one. Who is to say whether Tourvel's overt need to be
virtuous was any less profound than her secret attraction to
Valmont. It is simply because the second was concealed from
view that we cannot but take it more seriously. Despite an
intellectual recognition that secrecy and profundity are not
necessarily the same thing, our essentialist minds leap on revelations as the deeper truth. We just can't help give less credit
to clearly advertised motives. So nothing less than disclosure,
or even better discovery, will do, even if this is an unfair trick
of psychology. Here the fact of revelation, of a secret shared,
creates the conditions under which a connection can feel like
an intimate one: why it is a furtive force.

The fear of revelation

This is one reason why most encounters are not intimate. They do not have this defining property because people play safe. Exposure brings vulnerability and we learn that there is much to be gained in venturing nothing. The sad fact is that one can overcome those fences of privacy and not have the move accepted: have the bared cheek met with a slap or derision not a kiss or a smile. The shot falls wide, and shame is the price we pay. My intimacy with the barman requires that he accepts my knowing look in return: he determines that I've caught his private moment sympathetically and he is happy for me to be a confederate. If, by contrast, the barman catches my eye but glares at the intrusion, as if to say "none of your business", then he has rejected my offer of intimacy. Or if he feels embarrassed and turns away then the possibility of connection vanishes too.

There is always the chance, the likelihood even, that something will go wrong: a discord. The danger that comes from being unexpectedly revealed can create conditions for intimacy, but also for humiliation or anger. If in smiling back at my knowing smile he then realizes I'm in fact laughing at him, not with him, then the intimacy he thought we shared has been withdrawn, leaving him uncovered and vulnerable. The difficulty of taking genuine risks is that they may be met with harsh judgement, even in this trivial borderline case. Avert your eyes from the barman's gaze, hide the fact that you saw him with "civil inattention", and you don't have to risk him glaring at your intrusion.

So we have taboos and no-go areas. We avoid conversations that might make us uncomfortable, and that way keep intimacy out of reach. The sense of danger that comes from revelation is real enough. We might hope that an awkward truth revealed might be greeted with generosity and insight but there is every possibility that it will be used against us, or be misunderstood. And this makes intimacy fraught and unstable. This is why so many of those book titles talk of the struggles and fears that are embedded in the experience. No one wants to feel like Mr Bulstrode in *Middlemarch* confronted by the blackmailer Raffles, who walks back into his influential and reputable life with awkward knowledge of his past financial misdealings:

> The terror of being judged sharpens the memory: it sends an inevitable glare over that long unvisited past which has been habitually recalled only in general phrases … But intense memory forces a man to own his blameworthy past. With memory set smarting like a reopened wound, a man's is not simply a dead history, an outworn preparation of the present: it is not a repented error shaken loose from the life: it is a still quivering part of himself, bringing shudders and bitter flavours and tinglings of merited shame.

Without the potent gaze of someone who knows too much we can sweeten those bitter flavours, and recast those tingles of merited shame in a more flattering light. But this is exactly why intimacy demands the sense of an uncovering.

Being judged may create terror but there is the promise of relief too: that instead of taking advantage the other person will be kind.

We vary in the degree of safety we require and equally vary in our capacity for intimacy, but not in a straightforward way. So we create a subtle ballet of edging forwards and back: testing the waters with double entendre, half hearing, veiled speech and plausible deniability. Roger Brown, the social psychologist who spent his later years risking his reputation cruising in public toilets for assignations with young men, would describe the subtle slide of the foot under the cubicle door: just enough to register possible interest, not enough to remove reasonable doubt.

With the removal of doubt you can't take it back and are stuck with the threat of merited shame. Steven Pinker has a detailed analysis of this tendency in *The Stuff of Thought*, in which he uses a scene from the film *When Harry Met Sally*. After Sally has finished calculating her portion of the bill Harry just stares at her:

Harry: (smiling) You're a very attractive person.
Sally: (suspicious) Thank you.
Harry: Amanda never said how attractive you were.
Sally: Well, maybe she doesn't think I'm attractive.
Harry: I don't think it's a matter of opinion. Empirically, you are attractive.
(Sally gets up.)
Sally: (astonished) Amanda is my friend.
Harry: So?

Sally: So, you're going with her.

Harry: So?

Sally: So, you're coming on to me.

Harry: No I wasn't. (With disbelief, she stares at him.)

Harry: What? Can't a man say a woman is attractive without it being a come-on? All right, all right. Let's just say, just for the sake of argument, that it was a come-on. What do you want me to do about it? I take it back, OK? I take it back.

Sally: You can't take it back.

Harry: Why not?

Sally: Because it's already out there.

Harry: Oh jeez. What are we supposed to do? Call the cops? It's already out there!

We spend much time and energy making sure we can take back what has been said. Caution impedes the possibility of intimacy because it prevents the *mutual* knowledge described in the previous section. What does this mean? It means that with mere *individual* knowledge, where I know something and you know something but I can't be sure that you know that I know, we still have the protection of plausible deniability. But in the recursive explosion of mutual knowledge there is no pretending it never happened, because I know and you know and I know that you know that I know ... Most approaches to intimacy are subtle for exactly this reason. How many of us have agonized over the wording in an email so that we show enough interest without being so explicit we can't take it back? Much comedy (picture *Fawlty Towers*, *The Office* or *Borat* as examples) turns on people making misjudgements and the consequences that follow from those.

The unexpected limits of trust

So the conspiracy needs a great deal of trust. Think of the etymology of confide (Latin *con* and *fidere*, to trust): with faith. To be intimate requires that we are confident enough to confide our confidences to a confidant: for your eyes only. I need to be confident that you won't misuse the power you have over me now that I have revealed myself. And trust has two dimensions. I need to trust your motivation (that you'll be on my side, that you won't betray me), but I also need to trust your competence (that you won't misunderstand what you've learned, or reveal it through negligence). In short, I need to believe that you are nice and in control too.

It is a staple of self-help that we need to "open up" to experience intimacy. In its suggestion that secrets are bad for us and things are "better out than in" the implication of self help is that privacy is the enemy of intimacy. What is less often noted is an unpleasant corollary. If we are too open, if the fences are absent and there is no sense of discovery, the paradox is that this can banish intimacy too. While self-disclosure is a key stepping stone towards another person we can easily go too far and keep the other at bay by surrendering our privacy in too wholesale a manner.

In his paper "Privacy and Intimacy", Avrum Geurin Weiss argues that privacy is an important part of intimacy. He quotes one of his patients: "it enables me to be intimate and have an identity. Before, I've been so concerned with intimacy or with relationship that I was throwing away the identity and confusing fusion with mutuality or intimacy" (1987: 122).

Weiss quotes Brown, who describes intimacy as "a dance of courtship", now moving closer and now further away:

> The prerequisite for "letting someone in" is the certain knowledge that one can "keep them out" and – if need be – "throw them out" if they prove ungracious. Thus, the best playgrounds have fences, and a secure gate, which one can open or close at will and lock if necessary.
>
> (Quoted in *ibid.*: 123)

Intimacy is bound up in the feeling of discovery to such a degree that couples who have no more secrets to share can suddenly lose the capacity for intimate experience. Barthes continues the aside quoted at the beginning of this chapter to illustrate the worry: "I knew everything, immediately, about Y's desires, hence Y himself was obvious to me, and I was inclined to love him no longer in a state of terror but indulgently, the way a mother loves her child" (2002: 134).

This comment warns us to be careful what we wish for. If you know someone too well their capacity to hold your attention in a certain way may vanish. And this may be a problem for intimacy for the reason that those fences need to be overcome. Their sheer absence removes the possibility of discovery, which is so necessary to experiencing connection.

And this can be a real problem for couples over time. One of the apparent benefits of longer-term relationships is that there is no problem being explicit about saying what you want from each other. You can say to your partner, like Harry and Sally's friends who get married and feel that relief, "please tell me I don't have to be out there again". Long-term partners can say of and to each other things that courting couples wouldn't dream of. Their backstage regions are available to each other, fully lit up, and there is less reason and space to hide. But there is less to uncover too.

To reiterate, while "intimacy" depends on the *sense* of revelation it doesn't and cannot depend on full, actual revelation. This is not only because we are fearful of revealing ourselves fully, but also because we can't. We don't know most of what drives us, and those motives themselves are sometimes fleeting and unformed so as to be outside the range of expression. But it cannot exist without *some* revelation either. We are fickle in our need for just enough disclosure. Too little, and we pass by each other in our highly defended armour; too much transparency, and we start to pass through each other.

We dance around too much and too little disclosure, but on the whole we suffer from too little. In this book intimacy is an exception to the rule. The rule is that we are isolate, incurious, playing safe or not paying enough attention. And to be too safe is to impede the possibility of a genuinely intimate encounter. We need mechanisms that free us of the accusation of manipulation or tactics, and we need genuinely to feel the significance of the connection. This is why intimacy must also be emotionally heightened.

6

Unruly Emotion

Our emotions show us to ourselves. While our verbal accounts are filled with generalizing conventions (I'm a Capricorn, an extrovert, a mother, something in the city), our emotional expressions support a more textured self-knowledge. When I feel indignant, or envious, or excited, or disgusted, or proud, I get a richer insight into my character, my aesthetic and moral preoccupations, than when I just hear what I say to people about myself. Sometimes my emotional reactions will show me things about myself that I like, such as being moved by an unprovoked act of kindness between strangers. And sometimes I discover things about myself that I don't like, as did Eva Katchadourian in *We Need to Talk About Kevin* when she first encountered her newborn son:

Dr Rhinestein dangled the infant over my breast and rested the tiny creature down with … painstaking gentleness. Kevin was damp, and blood creased his neck, the crooks of his limbs. I put my hands diffidently around him. The expression on his twisted face was disgruntled. His body was inert; I could only interpret his lassitude as a lack of enthusiasm …

And all the while I was waiting. My breath shallow, I was waiting. And I kept waiting. *But everybody says–*, I thought. And then distinctly: *Beware of what "everybody says"*

Franklin [her husband], I felt – absent. I kept scrabbling around in myself for this new *indescribable* emotion, like stirring a crowded silverware drawer for the potato peeler, but no matter how I rattled around, no matter what I moved out of the way, it wasn't there.

This literary echo of Madame Bovary bending over the cot and whispering to herself "how ugly this child is", reminds us that we often don't feel things that line up with what we are expected to feel. And yet, whether the insights are welcome or not, this emotion-laden route to self-knowledge is an important element in our chances of an intimate connection with others.

Emotion in our current usage of the term is a relatively recent part of the human self-image. The *Oxford English Dictionary* traces the changing definition of the term and clearly reveals a gradual shift in its usage from the realm of action to the realm of feeling. The current "psychological" meaning is given as originating in the late eighteenth century: "A mental 'feeling' or 'affection' (e.g. of pleasure of pain, desire or aversion, surprise, hope or fear, etc.), as distinguished from cognitive or volitional states of consciousness. Also abstr. 'feeling' as distinguished from the other classes of mental phenomena."

With the rise of emotions as inner drivers of human behaviour, coinciding with the rise of the new discipline of psychology, came a turning point of great significance. It became possible to see emotion as both the provider of human goals (hopes, fears, desires) and the propulsive force towards them.

Despite this, emotion, and its antecedents such as passions or humors, have had a mixed press over time. A rationalist tradition in the history of science and philosophy has tried to keep it on the unruly margins. This influential view has overshadowed our self-image since Plato identified reason as a charioteer battling to control the wild horses of spirit and appetite. As he summarized it, "if the better elements of the mind which lead to order and philosophy prevail, then they pass their life here in happiness and harmony, masters of themselves" (*Phaedrus* 256a–b).

Self-mastery was the watchword of classical Greece and Rome. And, despite the resurgence of superstition and ignorance during the Dark Ages, this rationalist flame was reignited by key figures through the Renaissance and the Enlightenment, such as Francis Bacon and René Descartes, leading all the way up to twentieth-century psychological and economic views of the human mind as a thinking machine.

The proscription of emotion was not just a feature of scientific thinking but shaped moral imperatives over time. For

Christians, people have a sacred duty to God to overcome their short-term needs and desires. For utilitarians such as Bentham, Mill and Henry Sidgwick, our duties to others are to fall out of a "felicific calculus" so as to maximize happiness, rather than anything to do with sympathy or sentiment. For Kant, our moral code should be governed instead by the logic of a "categorical imperative"; only act in a way that is consistent with a maxim you would elevate into a universal law. For all these moral traditions, emotion is a distraction at best and bad for us at worst. Rodin's sculpture of *The Thinker* seems to embody this ideal and strongly echoes one architect of this tradition, Descartes, and his *cogito*, "I think therefore I am".

Certainly emotion was not a priority in this picture, overshadowed as it was by grander moral and theoretical strictures. Heads should rule hearts. And there are ongoing strands of this tradition running through our culture today. Phrases such as "you're just being emotional" imply that your judgement is impaired while you are in this heightened state. On this view emotions are childish things, to be put away as we grow older and wiser.

Yet contrary to the influential view that we walk around like a head on a stick, it has become clear enough that human beings are mired in emotion. It fuels our motives and colours our characters. The historical counterpoint to the rationalist tradition, even if it had to battle from the margins, is the claim that we are nothing without emotion. It was Hume (an Enlightenment contemporary of Kant's) who claimed that "reason is, and ought only to be the slave of the passions"

The Thinker (1902), Auguste Rodin (photograph © Daniel Stockman (Flickr: Paris 2010 Day 3 - 9), CC-BY-SA-2.0 [http://creativecommons.org/licenses/by-sa/2.0], via Wikimedia Commons).

(*Treatise* 2.3.3.4). For Hume nothing has value, there is no point to action, without emotion. In the same vein his Scottish contemporary Adam Smith advocated the image of an expansive sympathetic self that resonates to and is constituted by the needs of others. Similarly Jean-Jacques Rousseau's romanticism of the same period, based on the idea that we should favour the untrammelled expression of emotion over reason, has its apotheosis in a modern therapeutic culture where talking cures help to reach the innocent child, or the noble savage, within.

While emotion has a lesser pedigree in the history of human self-understanding it is fast coming up on the rails. Even modern economics has finally discovered emotion (a moment often cited as happening in 2002, when Daniel Kahneman became the first psychologist to win the Nobel Prize in Economics). This is due to a gradual recognition that rational models were not cut out to predict actual human behaviour. Contrary to the previous view that we are all rational utility optimizers busily responding to incentives, it seems that *Homo sapiens* does not resemble that mythical variant *Homo economicus* quite so much. A neat illustration of this comes from the "ultimatum game".

John and Jane have never met and will never meet again. John receives £10, and is told to share it with Jane as he sees fit, leaving Jane either to accept the deal or reject it; she can't negotiate (hence the ultimatum). If she rejects it then neither of them gets anything. Objectively the most self-interested and *rational* deal is for John to keep £9 and offer Jane £1. After all, this is better than nothing for Jane so she shouldn't, in theory, reject it. She does though! In fact, because John knows this, the average offer tends to be around £4. From an economist's standpoint this is more generous than is necessary but is in fact the minimum that John can get away with, since when he goes for less Jane will reject the offer, forgoing a real benefit in order to punish him for his greediness. She doesn't want to be dissed.

This empirical result varies across cultures but the general message is that the rational story won't do. And so thanks to results like this, the view that emotions need to be central rather than peripheral to understanding human beings has become established lately as unarguable.

In truth both strands exist within our culture today and each can lead to a cartoon version. Kant's path leads to Mr Spock on *Star Trek* and Hume's leads to lurid confessions on daytime television. These strands intertwine in British culture, which on the one hand is influenced by the US model of consumption and therapy, while on the other hand preserves a self-image of restraint and diffidence. And since cultures police and shape the way our emotions are allowed to be expressed, we lurch between too much and too little – damned if we do, damned if we don't – oscillating between poles of constipation and incontinence.

But why does intimacy need to be emotionally charged or heightened? It seems to me that there are two reasons. The first is that emotion concentrates our minds; it is an indication that something matters to us, and that we care. So, unsurprisingly, the grounds for intimacy are best established when the two people are in a heightened state. This can be created through a shared sense of threat, a shared response to beauty or novelty, the reckless bonding that can be triggered by alcohol (one of the reasons that drinking is so popular), shocking good news, a terrible loss. Both people have to be wide awake, not sleepwalking through habit and familiarity. This is not to say these emotions need to be *expressed* strongly, but they do need to be *felt* on both sides and expressed aptly. Otherwise intimacy slides back into familiarity without the appropriate vibrato. We shall return later to the skill involved in reading others' emotions and how crucial that is in sensing what matters to them.

The second key feature of emotion is that it is not entirely within our control. Our emotions, the capacity for hatred, guilt, joy, love, anger, excitement and so on, play a key role in enabling us to believe each other. They enable the conditions of trust because they are hard to fake, or to deploy tactically, and so become guarantors of sincerity. And we distrust people whose emotional range seems out of place with the situation at hand. There is little so discomfiting to us than someone obviously faking an emotional reaction. In the film *Broadcast News*, William Hurt plays a news journalist who makes his breakthrough when interviewing a rape victim, and is apparently moved to tears by her story. We are repelled to see, however, that he has staged the whole thing. Genuine emotion is an enabler of intimacy then because the very helplessness it creates makes us vulnerable and believable.

Helplessness

Do emotions overwhelm us because they are wired into us? Is that deep-seated ancient part of our brains known as the limbic system undermining the best efforts of our more controlled prefrontal cortex? Is that "seething cauldron of desires" that Freud called the Id always going to play havoc with the Ego's hope for mastery? There does seem to be underlying emotional weather that applies to anyone, regardless of context. The argument made by cultural universalists, such as the psychologist Paul Ekman, is that there are six major emotional categories that exist in all humans: happiness, sadness, anger, fear, disgust and surprise. These are deep-seated, evolved capacities, identifiable on facial expressions of people from diverse cultures. No human can be without these basic emotions, and they are not learned. Blind babies start to smile or frown without ever having seen those expressions on another face. This creates a universal substrate that can link any humans together on a fundamental level, regardless of cultural context.

Ekman has attempted to extend the theory to capture a more subtle and comprehensive emotional array, including amusement, contempt, contentment, embarrassment, excitement, guilt, pride in achievement, relief, satisfaction, sensory pleasure and shame. The point of the universalists' claim is that for all our need to express emotions aptly or carefully, the fact that they are wired into us limits the control we may have over whether we feel them and how to display them. In this sense, to some extent, we all wear our hearts on our sleeves.

89

On the other hand, notwithstanding this common substrate, there are clearly many emotions that cannot be said to be wired into us. There is a difference between the universal capacity to smile when pleased and the sardonic, mocking smile of a patronizing, false friend. These more sophisticated, context-specific emotions have been shaped by the cultures we inhabit and may mark us off from each other more than the universalist might like. A vivid if *outré* example of this sort is the "state of being a wild pig" that is experienced among young men of the Gururumba tribe in New Guinea. In this state these men run wild, stealing things from friends and strangers, and often attacking bystanders at random. The emotion is most commonly experienced by young men, between the ages of twenty-five and thirty-five, and is tolerated despite its antisocial elements, which can give them some leeway at a time they have to confront the financial and marital responsibilities of young adulthood. Clearly this is not a universally evolved feature of all humans.

And yet, even if the claim is that many emotions are shaped by culture, it does not follow that one has more control over how to display them. A young Gururumba man being a wild pig feels it as strongly as anyone else experiencing a rush of fear. That's why people in his community tolerate it; they know there is not much he can do about it.

So whether emotions are biologically given or constructed culturally, whether they are clear and present or obscure and subtle, they are not easily deployed on the basis of reasoning. This is important to the experience of intimacy because that very helplessness is a sign of sincerity. We established in

Chapter 5 that intimacy depends on a high degree of trust. Emotions are guarantors of this trustworthiness to some degree. If I am inclined to feel guilty, rather than merely follow a prescription of loyalty, *pace* Kant, you have more reason to trust me not to betray you. To have an emotion, whether wired into us genetically or inculcated through social norms, is to be, in a sense, had by it. To some extent it must be obeyed.

Seeing around the sides

So emotions are designed to enhance our credibility by being hard to fake, which gives us reasons to do just that, hard as it may be. Politeness is a never-ending example of how we modify our emotional expression. "That's amazing, thanks!" we say on receiving an ill-chosen gift. This counterfeit emotion is largely conventional and not taken too seriously by most people. The classic example of this is the fake smile (first identified by the physician Guillaume Duchenne in the mid-nineteenth century) in which only the muscles around the mouth move while the muscles around the eyes (crucial for a genuine smile) refuse to participate. In this portrait of Duchenne himself (overleaf) we can see how the attempt to smile for the camera doesn't work if your eyes are not in on the act.

A genuine smile is now known as a Duchenne smile (which, ironically Duchenne fails to achieve in the image here). Many of us can see through fake emotion expression and not many of us can fake well. When we try the results are often comical,

91

Guillaume Duchenne

as anyone, watching the news coverage of the "extreme grief" performed by North Koreans on the death of Kim Jong-il, might have seen.

But these examples of consciously faking emotion are less significant than the more disturbing but much more common unconscious version. The best liars, after all, have convinced themselves first. This more common form of bad faith occurs when we leap on to the clichéd version of what we ought to be feeling without attending to the complexity of what we are actually feeling. This is nicely brought out in a moment from *The Sportswriter*, the first of Richard Ford's trilogy about the life of Frank Bascombe (the eponymous sportswriter). In this first novel he is recovering from the death of his son and the consequent collapse of his marriage. He develops a relationship with Vicki, who maddens him with a shallow fickleness. She is never quite able to commit to him and yet capable of surprising reversals too. In a telling scene they are meeting up ready for a weekend away. Frank has just had his hopeful smile well met by Vicki, who in an affectionate lurch, says she'd marry him "any time". This is more than he could have hoped for. And he asks:

And I feel exactly what at this debarking moment?
At least a hundred things at once, all competing to take the moment and make it their own, reduce undramatic life to a gritty, knowable kernel.
This, of course, is a minor but pernicious lie of literature, that at times like these, after significant or disappointing divulgences, at arrivals or departures of obvious importance, when touchdowns are scored, knock-outs recorded, loved ones buried, orgasms notched, that at such times we are any of us altogether in an emotion, that we are within ourselves and not able to detect other emotions we might also be feeling, or be about to feel, or prefer to feel. If it's literature's job to tell the truth about these moments, it usually fails, in my opinion, and it's the writer's fault for falling into such conventions.

Frank's curse, and gift, is his ability to see around the sides of his emotions, rather than completely inhabit them. This means they lose their persuasive force, because he can't, as we say, "lose himself in the moment". He is right to say that literature's lie is occasionally to show us a simpler story. I shall come later to the question whether this lie is ubiquitous or even that pernicious in the final chapter. And he is right to say life is not that simple (a beautiful irony of Ford's novels is his capacity to show literary characters who refuse to submit to literary conventions and can speak to their limits).

Seeing around the sides of our emotions can impede intimacy, as it did for Frank when faced with an affectionate Vicki, but there are complementary dangers in surrendering to emotion too easily. Surrendering to emotion is a problematic notion for various reasons. First, there are many controlling conditions in play because emotions have a social reality. Our reactions, for example, are closely tied to how we frame a situation; as threatening, as exciting, as dull, and so on. Picture a charismatic speaker working a crowd into a frenzy of aggression. If someone has perceived authority they can frame situations and shape the general sense of what an apt expression of emotion might be. Maybe that North Korean wailing was not so fake after all. So we have some responsibility for which emotion seems apt in a situation and can also manage our own and others' emotions to a degree, whether soothing someone's fears, turning them on or making them angry.

Another problem with untrammelled expression is that emotions aren't always clearly delineated. There are many ways we can get the story of what we are feeling quite wrong. Emotion provides a constant threat to our integrity, and often creates the bad faith of self-deception. This is partly because feelings are such blunt signals of our emotional range. In *A Grief Observed*, C. S. Lewis comments how little idea he had that grief would feel so much like fear. We know that the sweating palms of love and anxiety are interchangeable to some degree.

It may seem odd to think we don't always know what we are feeling, yet there is plenty of evidence to support this awkward insight. One classic experiment in the 1970s had young men walking across a hazardously swaying bridge with low handrails over a deep ravine. They were asked by a female researcher to fill out a survey and given her phone number for any follow-up questions they may have had about the research project. The crucial difference was when they were approached. In the first condition the men were asked after they had safely crossed over to the other side and in the second condition they were asked when they were halfway across the ravine. The striking outcome was that in the second condition the men were far more likely to call the researcher a few days later (often asking for a date). The experimenters, Donald Dutton and Arthur Aron, concluded that they had confused their state of high arousal on the bridge (due to fear) with being aroused by the researcher. After all even hate can look like a perverse form of love.

Not only can we see around the sides of our emotions or misread them, but we can also get sentimentally lost in them thanks to a helping of fictions that pull away from reality. For everyone who looks inside themselves and feels nothing at a funeral, there are those who cannot help seeing themselves. In *The Unbearable Lightness of Being*, Milan Kundera describes this experience as kitsch. Towards the end of the novel he describes a man stopping his car to watch children running along the grass surrounding an ice rink. "Just look at them", he says. "Now that's what I call happiness." Kundera asks how he could possibly know this is happiness: "Could he see into their souls?"

In the realm of kitsch, the dictatorship of the heart reigns supreme …

Kitsch causes two tears to flow in quick succession. The first tear says: how nice to see children running on the grass!

The second tear says: how nice to be moved, together with all mankind, by children running on the grass!

All this makes emotion quite unstable terrain. We know we need its genuine experience and expression to have an intimate connection and so we sometimes try too hard and reach for a substitute. Kitsch helps to tie it down with ribbons or keep it safe in a chocolate box, but this is to make it inert.

The more genuine, but arduous route involves living with emotional uncertainty: sometimes becoming too sentimental, sometimes too cold. So it is for the other person. But not everyone has the gifts of interpretation, what these days is called emotional intelligence, to pick up the changing signals. Despite the risks of bad faith we can and must tutor our emotions to some degree or at least suppress (or sometimes exaggerate) their expression. The apt expression of emotion is always going to be something more, or less, than a straight outpouring of feeling. We need not only to have the right emotions in the circumstances, but to express them in the right kind of way. Expressing the appropriate emotion in the appropriate way is much easier said than done, thanks partly to the changing norms in our culture. This makes for a challenging environment in which to express emotion aptly.

The right kind of expression

We connect emotion to temperature: its absence to cold-ness and its abundance with being overheated. But, unlike Goldilocks's sampling of the three bears' porridge, it is hard to know when the temperature is "just right". The histori-cal ambivalence of Western culture does not help too much with deciding on particular cases. One person's florid, self-indulgent melodrama is another's genuine and sincere out-pouring. One person's subtle expression, muted in its pastel shades, indicating how deep those still waters run, appears to another as frigid, inexpressive or detached. So expressing emotion takes skill and sensitivity to context.

We must feel emotion in the right way if we are to expe-rience intimacy. But unless we can express it well this will still be an impediment. People vary hugely in their emotional intelligence and their ability to find the right words. Some peo-ple suffer from "alexithymia": literally the absence of words to describe emotional states, which is hard enough to do when we *know* what we are feeling. But as Frank Bascombe was honest enough to recognize, we often are obscure to our-selves. The psychologist Daniel Gilbert explores this theme in *Stumbling on Happiness*:

Some people seem to be keenly aware of their moods and feelings, and may even have a novelist's gift for describing their every shade and flavour. Others of us come equipped with a somewhat more basic emotional vocabulary that, much to the chagrin of our romantic partners, consists primarily of *good, not so good* and *I already told you.*   (2007: 62)

In a crisis, or in situations when people are under pressure, we can see an exaggerated version of how strangers can achieve intimacy if they have sufficient emotional dexterity. The skill required can be seen in emergencies where professional helpers need to enable those they help to retain their dignity. An example comes from a mountain-rescue group who would often see people in unflattering "backstage" conditions and so need to be able to handle embarrassment with what Goffman calls "protective practices" such as tacitly refuting claims, made by the rescued, of stupidity (Lois 2001). Gary and Lois, two of the mountain-rescue team in question, *neutralized embarrassment* in a hiker who had twisted her ankle by accepting her justifications for getting lost, and making up new ones (the path is poorly marked, loads of people get lost here) so as to fix her "spoiled identity" and more efficiently assess her medical condition. They offered "hints" by frontloading a conversation about what is to be discussed, thus heading off any need for explanation or self-deprecation.

Goffman comments more generally on the nature of farewells, which, among other things, "show what the participants may expect of one another when they next meet". The airport is so often the place where the little deaths of departure are visible to others: the long, tear-stained embrace versus the peremptory turn on the heel. This is a good way to see how intimate *encounters* can form the bedrock of intimate *relationships*. Stringing together these experiences can be cumulative, but not necessarily; after each one the chance of another is somewhat heightened or weakened. One might hope for more but this is unpredictable emotional weather. In *Four Weddings and a Funeral* it is very hard for Charles (Hugh Grant) to know the basis on which he and Carrie (Andie McDowell) will next meet. Each intimate encounter they have (in the context of her getting married or being married) is filled with intensity but left quite ambiguous in the end. It is clear that he wants more but quite unclear what she wants. His heart is filled with vague hope, his head telling him to "expect nothing". This motif of the man pursuing the love of a mercurial woman is well known through literature and film. *Swann in Love* (the short novel that is part 2 of *Swann's Way*, the first volume of Marcel Proust's *In Search of Lost Time*) is an intense and subtle meditation on all the agonies that attend love turned sour and obsessive by jealousy, with constant references to it as a sickness. Swann is doomed because he will never get a reliable signal in return. Yet he must risk that pain if he is to hope for the connection he seeks.

The virtue of submission

What Frank Bascombe is saying, and what he says literature should be reminding us, is that we should be distrustful of the epiphanic revelation: that we shouldn't be too seduced by the feeling of being certain. And yet if we are to hold back enough to see around the sides of it, there is also possibly something missing. Being confused is one thing. Holding back, not to allow the emotion to overcome, is a way of refusing the possibility of intimacy. Of course the emotion could be mis-described, or it could be triggered by something we decry after the event. How many drunken outbursts of "I love you" to an equally drunk friend look ridiculous the next morning? Nevertheless, without the capacity to lose oneself in an emotion, however trite and clichéd (they are designed as blunt indicators in any case) it is hard to know how to trust. The revelation of emotion without too much control creates the conditions for trust.

It is no good for intimacy to be too skilled at seeing around the sides of your emotions. It might be wiser, on some level, to do so and to be sure of avoiding lapsing into kitsch but that very worry will keep intimacy at bay. If intimacy is our goal we need to risk looking like fools and let the emotion hold sway. The point is to be had by them sufficiently to convey first that you mean what you say you feel, and second that this is not entirely up to you. Anger, passionate love, fear and shame all have the characteristics of sincerity in that they are hard to deploy tactically and hard to conceal. Intimacy needs this fuel.

The weakening of explicit emotional expression over time is one of the reasons it can be hard to sustain intimacy in long-term relationships. Susan Sontag describes the phenomenon well. In early September 1956, living in Cambridge, Massachusetts as a graduate student in philosophy at Harvard University, when her son David was almost four and her husband Philip Rieff was teaching at Brandeis, she recorded her thoughts on the matter. "Whoever invented marriage", she wrote:

was an ingenious tormentor. It is an institution *committed* to the dulling of the feelings. The whole point of marriage is repetition. The best it aims for is the creation of strong, mutual dependencies.

Quarrels eventually become pointless, unless one is always prepared to act on them – that is, to end the marriage. So, after the first year, one stops "making up" after quarrels – one just relapses into angry silence, which passes into ordinary silence, and then one resumes again.   (Sontag & Rieff 2008: 81)

Long-term relationships often become too safe for intimacy. When people talk of renewing the relationship, with second honeymoons or a fresh start, they often underestimate this aspect. The fact of emotional safety does not sit well with the possibility of intimacy. Margaret Schlegel, for all her pragmatism, was the one to articulate the need we have; "only connect" requires not playing safe. One of the ways she could express this hope was through her recognition that we must not over-prepare for life. We should not have that knowing buffer that kept Frank Bascombe from entering the moment wholly. Here is a scene where Margaret is rejecting advice from Mrs Munt, who argues that in love and life "It's as well to be prepared":

"No – it's as well not to be prepared."
 "Because –"
Her thought drew being from the obscure borderland. She could not explain in so many words, but she felt that those who prepare for all the emergencies of life

beforehand may equip themselves at the expense of joy.
It is necessary to prepare for an examination, or a dinner-
party, or a possible fall in the price of stock: those who
attempt human relations must adopt another method, or
fail. "Because I'd sooner risk it," was her lame conclusion.

…

"I hope to risk things all my life."
"Oh, Margaret, most dangerous."

This most dangerous path risking the emotional pain of
human relations is the one Frank Bascombe will never easily walk down. He holds himself apart and does not allow
the emotion to overwhelm him, but that way keeps intimacy
at bay. If, like Margaret, we take the more dangerous path,
then the hope is that it will be met with kindness rather than
hostility.

7

A Complicated Kindness

.

"I'm Gatsby," he said suddenly.

"What!" I exclaimed. "Oh, I beg your pardon."

"I thought you knew, old sport. I'm afraid I'm not a very good host."

He smiled understandingly – much more than understandingly. It was one of those rare smiles with a quality of eternal reassurance in it, that you may come across four or five times in life. It faced – or seemed to face – the whole eternal world for an instant, and then concentrated on you with an irresistible prejudice in your favour. It understood you just as far as you wanted to be understood, believed in you as you would like to believe in yourself, and assured you that it had precisely the impression of you that, at your best, you hoped to convey.

This "irresistible prejudice in your favour", this mixture of benevolence, generous spirit, understanding, seems to promise the possibility of intimate connection between Gatsby and Nick Carraway, the narrator of the novel and recipient of this wonderful smile. This is the kindness we look for in intimacy. If we can be sure of that "quality of eternal reassurance", we have just what we need to side with the Schlegel sisters' risk taking against Frank Bascombe's caution. In addition, where heightened emotion can become somewhat solipsistic, kindness is the counterbalancing force in achieving the mutualism of intimacy.

But can Nick trust that smile? Can we really know if all is as it seems? Gatsby appears to be the archetypal self-made man of the emergent modernist era, flickering in and out of focus throughout the novel. Is this smile an intimate one or a trick of the light? Is he making a promise or just being promising? By the end of the novel, Gatsby's emptiness is revealed, but at the start he stands for hope and enabled hopefulness in others. For all the risk taking that comes from searching for intimacy we will miss our mark if we are not met with kindness in return, and thus risk shame or humiliation.

But if intimacy always comes with kindness why do we fear it? Is the version I'm proffering a little sugary with good news? For instance, there is no reason to feel all perceptive people are kind. If the need for intimacy is about the need to be connected, to be understood, then maybe it comes as easily from an enemy as from a friend. Earlier I gave the example of how the relationship between O'Brien and Winston Smith in *1984* approaches intimacy but, it seems to me, crucially lacks the element of benevolence. But can we be so sure? What would Winston have said about it?

For the reciprocal part of intimacy to work it is enough to have that mutual knowledge. The sensitive and insightful with a talent for finding the right words may use that emotional intelligence to see around the sides of you, and so to humiliate you. And maybe that humiliation is all the more complete for being intimate. We all know people with a caricaturist's insight into other people's foibles or weak points. We talk of people who know what makes people tick, or have people "tapped"; these observers are capable of quite unwelcome insights because they know more than you want them to know and you know it too. Are there forms of intimacy that are similarly unwelcome, unkind, but intimate nonetheless?

We have seen that intimacy and shame are often connected. This is one of the reasons to fear intimacy after all. Shame means being uncovered when you are not ready to be and having nowhere to turn; the stigmatized self is left carrying an unholy weight. Maybe forced or unwelcome or unkind intimacy is intimacy nonetheless. Maybe someone who hates you can offer the flash of recognition that temporarily blots out the more solitary facts of life dulled into quiet by repetition and low expectations.

The relationship between enmity and deep knowledge is played out across many walks of life; picture chess grandmasters hunched over the board, probing each other's minds with exquisite care. Even in the most cerebral groves of academe Bertrand Russell saw fit to state: "I would rather be reported by my bitterest enemy among philosophers than by a friend innocent of philosophy" (1961: 101). One can see with that emotional intensity and deep, exclusive, mutual knowledge (all the other ingredients needed for intimacy) that this might be a far deeper form of connection than Susan Sontag's description of wedlock after the first year.

And yet I hold to the claim. Yes the near intimacy of enmity can be converted into intimacy itself. But that conversion, it seems to me, is brought about by the simple but crucial introduction of kindness. Without that catalyst we have torture. Stockholm syndrome for example, where hostages develop a deep bond with their captors, depends crucially on perceived acts of kindness toward the hostage.

I shall use another fictional example of violation and pain – soldiers fighting to the death – to make the claim that intimacy *does* require a certain kindness. Again a borderline case serves its purpose. The moment in question comes towards the end of the film *Saving Private Ryan* and is a particularly upsetting episode. The scene is set in a ruined French village where American soldiers are planning a last-minute and probably suicidal defence of a bridge against the heavily armed German forces. During the melée, in one of the bombed-out buildings, there is a hand-to-hand fight to the death between Private Mellish and an unnamed German soldier. During the desperate struggle Mellish pulls out his bayonet to attack the soldier but, as they struggle with the blade, is gradually overpowered by his stronger adversary who starts to turn his weapon against him. The final stage of the fight has the German pinning Mellish down with his body and in a position to force the bayonet into the latter's chest slowly as Mellish tries to resist. Mellish begs to live and pleads "you don't have to do this".

Do we see a glimpse of a certain kindness entering this most unlikely example of intimacy? I think we do. As the German soldier slowly stabs Mellish to death, he says: "Gib' auf, du hast keine Chance! Lass' es uns beenden! Es ist einfacher für dich, viel einfacher. Du wirst sehen, es ist gleich vorbei." This translates as: "Give up, you don't stand a chance! Let's end this here! It will be easier for you, much easier. You'll see it will be over quickly." In the final seconds their faces are very close and drips of sweat are falling off the German's face on to the American's. He quietly kills Mellish with "sh ..., sh ...", soothing him in his anguish. After killing Mellish he stands up exhausted, stained with sweat and blood, and walks round the corner to the staircase where he sees Corporal Upham (another American soldier whose job is to run ammunition to those who need it). Upham is paralysed by fear, the ammunition that would have saved Mellish's life draped around his neck, and sobbing. The German soldier looks at Upham with disgust and walks past him. This non-violent contempt provides a stark counterpoint to the genuine respect he felt for Mellish. This is consistent with a cinematic trope of mutually respectful eyes meeting in the heat of battle and the contempt those "who know" feel for the bureaucrats and cowards who leave them to do the dirty work. In their co-authored book *On Kindness*, Adam Phillips and Barbara Taylor go so far as to say genuine kindness depends on its ability to contain hostility.

The thing that works, [Donald] Winnicott says – the thing that makes relations between parents and children "feel real," in his phrase – is the hatred that is lived through without severing the relationship.   (2010: 93)

In fact, real kindness, real fellow feeling, entails hating and being hated – that is, really feeling available frustrations – and through this, coming to a more realistic relationship. This, one might say, is a more robust version of kindness, a kindness made possible through frustration and hatred rather than a kindness organized to repudiate (or to disown) such feelings. Kindness of this variety allows for ambivalence and conflict, while false, or magical, kindness distorts our perceptions of other people, often by sentimentalizing them, to avoid conflict. Sentimentality is cruelty by other means.   (*Ibid.*: 94)

It seems to me that in this final act of savagery there is a kindness borne out of respect and empathy for the other's plight ("there but for fortune go I") that emerges and starts to make that final moment an intimate one. His attacker is the last face that Mellish will ever see and, while it is a long way from a Gatsby smile, there may be a genuine sympathetic knowingness, a recognition with a trace of benevolence, that passes between them. It is precisely the ingredient that never occurs to O'Brien and is why the intimacy Winston was hoping for is a sham.

So it would be wrong to say we fear intimacy because it can be acutely shaming. Rather, we fear our hope for intimacy proving groundless. It is not that intimacy contains shame: quite the opposite. It is that even a near miss when we aim for intimacy can be acutely painful, although no longer intimate. But even if we can agree that intimacy requires kindness, we are left with the problems attendant on trying to be kind.

Killing with kindness

The Enlightenment insights of David Hume and Adam Smith led to the celebration of sympathy, or what they called "fellow feeling". Hume compared the transmission of emotion between people to the vibration of violin strings, with each individual resonating with the pains and pleasures of others as if they were his own. Smith said, "we become in some measure the same person … this is the source of fellow feeling" (2002: I.I.i.2–3).

But kindness is less of a vanilla conceit than we like to think. Nathaniel Hawthorne's pithy observation that "benevolence is the twin of pride" gives us some clue into the problem. Kindness and power are after all deeply interlinked. If I am to be kind to you then it is because you lack something I have the power to give. And this very fact can be fatal to our chances of an intimate connection. It doesn't have to be. Intimacy can survive a power imbalance, but it requires perceived goodwill on both sides to do so. The person in the position of strength needs to be forgiven for the power they have, and must acknowledge it with skill. Working out how to be kind is freighted, if unconsciously, with these judgements.

In *The Unbearable Lightness of Being*, Milan Kundera makes the interesting claim that even etymology can shape our capacity for the right type of kindness:

All languages that derive from Latin form the word "compassion" by combining the prefix meaning "with" (*com-*) and the root meaning "suffering" (Late Latin, *passio*). In other languages – Czech, Polish, German and Swedish, for instance – this word is translated by a noun formed of an equivalent prefix combined with the word that means "feeling". ...

The former like the versions of pity in French *pitie* and Italian *pieta* have something condescending about their usage.

"To take pity on a woman" means that we are better off than she, that we stoop to her level, lower ourselves.

   That is why the word "compassion" generally inspires suspicion. ...

For the other languages there is no connotation of inferiority on the part of the sufferer:

The secret strength of its etymology floods the word with another light and gives it a broader meaning: to have compassion (co-feeling) means not only able to live with the other's misfortune but also to feel with him any emotion – joy, anxiety, happiness, pain. This kind of compassion ... therefore signifies the maximal capacity of affective imagination, the art of emotional telepathy. In the hierarchy of the sentiments, then, it is supreme.

On one level it is easiest to give to others from a position of strength, since this means that one is giving charity for no strategic reason (one already has the strength to do without the gratitude of others). This is why we say you can judge someone by how they treat people who have no power over them. One of the reasons an unprovoked act of kindness is so moving is that it avoids the suspicion that this is a tactical move. Kindness from the relatively weak, someone who bends over backwards pandering to the boss, can be devalued because it looks like a play for favour or self-esteem.

But the problem with giving from a position of strength is that it can turn into another power play. Here kindness can turn into condescension. How often do we see the outstretched hand rejected with "I don't want your charity!"? And from the point of view of those who have power, it is easy to feel repelled by the unwanted generosity, pity or eager overinterest from others.

So giving (and in some sense taking back) is a complex and obscure task. If you buy drinks for your friends all night long, or always pay for dinner, and never accept anything in return, this creates the asymmetry where kindness undermines itself. We need to calibrate our reactions to allow reciprocity. The sociologist Richard Sennett describes this difficulty in his book *Respect*, in which he argues that reciprocity is the foundation of mutual respect:

Largesse complicates ... because it demonstrates the manipulative power of gift-giving. Even the freely given gift can injure the self-respect of the person to whom it is given, for "charity wounds" as the anthropologist Mary Douglas says; it lays a heavy burden of gratitude on the recipient, who may have nothing to give back but sub-mission. When compassion takes the form of pity, it can also demean the receiving party.   (2004: 149)

Even someone who chooses to give money to a cause, who will never know the identity of the recipient of their charity, will talk of "giving something back" and so invent the debt that they are in fact repaying. So if a gift, like lunch, is never free, we need to be very skilled in how we give and receive.

Careless or incontinent kindness can lead to the kind of idealization that undermines the first aspect of intimacy: mutual knowledge based on an accurate (although never perfectly accurate) understanding of the other. It is not good for connection to allow too much sentimentality or roman-ticism. Kindness uncorrected by truth is liable to lapse into something untrustworthy: an idealized mush. When Clive James lampooned his fellow critic Bernard Levin for being uncritically adulatory he summed it up with: "an encomium from Levin is a spray of treacle that leaves its object a shape-less mass" (James 1983: 40). If we are to avoid reducing each other to shapeless masses, we need to be faithful to the tex-ture of each other. So sometimes the kinder, as opposed to nicer, thing to do is to be truthful: to be as generous spirited as possible yet consistent with the facts. Consequently it is unwise to listen too well to flattery and pandering, which is why most of us have difficulty taking compliments, with their inbuilt test of our modesty. "You are too kind" is often the only rebuff. We can't easily trust flattery because words are so cheap, the limit point of this being represented by the oleaginous Uriah Heep.

Being able to give well takes skill, while needing to be unforced. If we hesitate before giving we can rob ourselves of appearing generous. Think of the person who pauses embarrassingly before getting up to buy their round. The same goes for being willing to receive. People today (men especially) are tutored by society to be strong and in control. This can seriously undermine their ability to accept kindness from another and so their ability to experience intimacy. As with the need to allow emotion to weaken one's control, we also need to allow ourselves to be recipients of others' generosity. And as a recipient we need not gush unconvincingly nor look our gift horse in the mouth. We need to be gracious as receivers and magnanimous as givers, finding the Aristotelian mean between vanity and humility.

Less can be more

Sometimes the kindest thing is to say nothing. There can be great power in understatement here. In the television series *Mad Men*, Don Draper epitomizes the persuasive power of the strong and silent type. An encomium from Draper is no spray of treacle. It is as laser clean as it is unexpected. Draper's charismatic skill comes from an unflinching gaze that won't shy from dislike and disappointment.

There is a key episode, "The Suitcase", where Don and Peggy stay up all night working, drinking, avoiding misery in the rest of their lives (for her an annoying boyfriend pressurizing her to come out for her birthday dinner, for him a phone call that he knows will bring terrible news), which leaves them, by the end, hand in hand, as intimately connected as we always suspected they could be. The episode starts inauspiciously with his searing critique of her suggested ad for Samsonite suitcases. Don says, "I'm glad you think you work in an environment where you are free to fail". He doesn't realize it is Peggy's birthday and she is quite stung by his severity. She then complains that he steals her ideas and never gives the credit

Don: It's your job. I give you money, you give me ideas.
Peggy: And you never say thank you.
Don: That's what the money is for!

Yet despite the harsh honesty and apparent inconsiderateness (he inadvertently demolishes her boyfriend's surprise dinner that evening), and despite the more overtly affectionate offers from others in the episode, Peggy chooses to spend time with Don because kindness from him matters all the more. When he finally takes that dreaded call at the end of their long night of drinking, working and sleeping on the couch in his office, he is in tears. She asks him why and he explains that someone who mattered very much to him has died. Who? she asks:

Don: The only person who ever knew me.
Peggy: That's not true.

Don has finally softened and allowed Peggy to see his vulnerability as well as to accept her reassurances, so as she places her hand over his the intimate link is made.

Phillips and Taylor explain how "Real kindness is an exchange with essentially unpredictable consequences. It is a risk precisely because it mingles our needs and desires with the needs and desires of others, in a way that so-called self-interest never can" (2010: 12). They go on to say that central to our humanity is "the ability to bear the vulnerability of others, and therefore of oneself … Indeed it would be realistic to say that what we have in common is our vulnerability; it is the medium of contact between us, what we most fundamentally recognize in each other … [Kindness will] open us up to the world [and worlds] of other people in ways that we both long for and dread" (*ibid.*: 10–11).

Paying attention

Intimacy, then, demands a type of kindness that specifies. Unlike Levin's spray of treacle it needs to hit its target, rather like buying someone a particularly apt present as opposed to some generic bit of tinsel. It is tempting to give and accept praise, which misses its mark: easy to give it because it takes effort and imaginative energy to get it right; and easy to accept because good news is tempting even if not strictly accurate.

There is a scene in *Middlemarch* where Will Ladislaw's eloquence is compared, by the politically ambitious but unimaginative Mr Brooke, with that of Edmund Burke, and Eliot comments:

> Will was not displeased with that complimentary comparison, even from Brooke; for it is a little too trying to human flesh to be conscious of expressing one's self better than others and never to have noticed, and in the general dearth of admiration for the right thing, even a chance bray of applause falling exactly in time is rather fortifying.

But if intimacy is what you are after then you need to pay more attention than that. Much of our ability to be appropriately kind to another person comes down to noticing. To pay attention is to avoid the unplanned callousness or even cruelty that can come from ignoring a cry for help, or turning someone into another version of themselves. Versions of ourselves, altering as they go from mouth to mouth, remind us of the obliviousness of other people.

If you don't pay attention you may not hear or, worse, you may mishear. It is sometimes better to be ignored entirely than to have what you have to say traduced, turned into cliché or, worse, into the opposite of what you mean. In order to pay attention well we need the kind of insights described in Chapter 5.

Notwithstanding all the complexities of kindness, its genuine and skilful expression can create that sense of feeling truly vindicated, especially when unexpected. In Miriam Toews's novel *A Complicated Kindness*, the alienated teenager Nomi Nickel is visiting her dying friend in hospital and is appalled by the way her friend is being looked after. She encounters a harsh and judgemental nurse, who asks her to leave. After losing her temper and throwing a carton of juice at the nurse, she agrees to go.

> On my way out I stopped at the nurses' desk and asked the nice one, the one who'd asked me to leave but to come back soon *when the dust has settled*, if they could please take good care of my friend and cook her food a little longer and keep the room warm and things off her stomach and the nurse nodded and smiled and assured me that she would try. She told me the short-tempered nurse was under a lot of stress and that next time I was upset about something I should see her, not the short-tempered nurse, personally, and we could try to fix it up. I wanted not to be overwhelmed by her kindness because it made me sad to be so happy about something like that but on the way out, walking into the sunshine, I felt like my chest was going to explode and I looked straight into the sun to give me something painful to concentrate on.

Modern society, according to Phillips and Taylor, elevates and idealizes kindness into "a virtue so difficult to sustain that only the magically good can manage it" — this "destroys people's faith in real or ordinary kindness" (2010: 58). But, as they want to assure us, real and ordinary kindness *does* exist. "We depend on each other not just for our survival but for our very being", they argue in their final chapter. "The self without sympathetic attachments is either a fiction or a lunatic" (*ibid*.: 97)

PART TWO

Barriers to Intimacy

To paraphrase Ernest Jones's comment about love (in his *Papers on Psycho-Analysis*), "there is much less intimacy in the world than there appears to be". Jones made his comment at a time when the ideals of human connection were being undermined by Freud's new theories, which showed how divided people were against themselves and from each other. If anything, over the following decades, with the advent of pop music, advertising and Hollywood, a gap between popular imagery and psychological reality has widened. The idea of intimacy is talked about and reinforced in so many ways we could be forgiven for believing it is within easy reach and therefore disappointed to feel it is more readily available to others (even to a dog, a cat and a mouse in a well-known British Gas advert) than ourselves. After all, the rise of social-networking sites puts hundreds of "friends" within a click of a mouse. The illusions belie the truth that intimacy is rare, elusive and short-lived for most of us, for most of the time.

Meanwhile, our ambition to experience intimacy is as strong as ever. A social animal can't help but feel that prolonged separateness is the source of anxiety and, for the psychoanalyst Erich Fromm, it leads to shame and guilt because separateness leaves one unable to use human faculties, helplessly unable to grasp the world and so defenceless to its depredations: "The deepest need of man, then, is the need to overcome his separateness, to leave the prison of his aloneness" (Fromm 2010: 9). And the corollary question is "the question of how to overcome separateness, how to achieve union, how to transcend one's individual life and find at-onement" (*ibid.*)

While it is true that few things are more important than knowing someone and feeling known by them in return, the key relationships in which we might hope to find intimacy are those that exist over time: that offer a deepening of mutual knowledge such as between lovers or friends, or within families. While the chance of experiencing intimacy is not limited to these relationships, in each of these there resides that tantalizing promise.

Yet no relationship is consistently intimate, and perhaps most are not intimate at all. Crucially, intimate *relationships* not only have had many and various intimate *exchanges* but they contain the promise of more to come too. Much of the time relationships merely simulate intimacy; convention demands it. And we simulate intimacy so well it is hard to distinguish a genuinely intimate encounter from the fake Valentine's Day version. We have all the cultural material at our disposal. Yet, to repeat, most relationships, like that of Margaret and Mr Wilcox in *Howards End*, are frustrated by the absence of intimacy.

In this part I want to look at some of the barriers to intimacy that we experience in everyday life. What stops the self and the other from truly connecting? These impediments occur at various levels, whether involving personal insecurities of the self, lack of imagination towards the other person, the wishful thinking that creates too false a convergence between people and an aversion towards conflict, as well as inhibiting contexts of various kinds. These range from lacking the close-up convenience of occupying the same space with room and time for those delicate threads of connection to spin out and the muted tones to be heard (that's why people call the archetypal candle-lit dinner "intimate") all the way to larger cultural norms that prevent or distort our need for connection in the first place.

8

Insecurities

Intimacy makes us happy because it helps us to feel truly justified. This was something I described in detail in my book *The Happiness Paradox*. To feel justified is to have that feeling of recognition, applause, acknowledgement, acceptance in a way that is consonant with who we are in all our strangeness. Intimacy provides a peculiarly intense form of justification.

Stendhal's observation that "Everything can be acquired in solitude, except character" reminds us that in order to feel justified in this way one cannot do it alone. It depends on validating recognition from another. But anyone else will not do. The other person needs to be a *potent* audience if the justification is going to be worth having. Adoring fans, uncritical adulation, blind loyalty all fall short. As for comedians standing in front of a live audience, the cheering only means something to us if it comes with the risk of jeering. Canned laughter is not enough.

And because "intimacy" implies something secret and important revealed, it brings vulnerability through risk of exposure. An exposed cheek might be kissed, or slapped. I can picture a scene in the television programme *The West Wing* between Josh Lyman and his boss Leo McGarry, two of the Whitehouse senior staff, who have a very close and affectionate conversation, after which Leo appears to put his arms out as if to say "we're fine". On cue Josh leans in for a hug, but Leo springs back and asks "What are you doing?" The toe-curling embarrassment is a reminder to Josh not to be so blithe in future.

This means you can share intimacy only with someone who has the power to hurt you, in the sense that those hopeful efforts, if they miss their mark, can turn to shame or embarrassment, or worse. The fear of rejection, ridicule or humiliation is the undertow of the hope for intimacy. And by the same token, unwanted attempts at intimacy can create the corollary feelings of guilt, irritation, boredom, hostility and even revulsion in the recipient. This is why the uncanny term reverberates with depth and significance.

This is also why, for most of the time in human relations, caution is our watchword and with it we keep intimacy at bay. Our desires are hidden in conventions of plausible deniability, and indirect or veiled speech. "No, don't worry, that's fine, I was busy anyway." We focus on the practical, the conversations that work at a safe distance, and don't test ourselves because we are anxious about what a test might reveal. To break out into the open is fraught with risk.

But not everyone assesses these risks in the same way. Different temperaments and different life histories will shape the confidence with which we might stick out our necks in the first place. Yes, too much insecurity will put intimacy out of reach, but not everyone is so insecure. A lot of academic research suggests that our personality types are, to a large extent, framed by a combination of genetic inheritance and early environmental influences. Much of this work is drawn together in an umbrella theory known to psychologists as "the big five" factor personality theory. The claim is that there are five dimensions on which we differ from each other but remain somewhat invariant over time and across different contexts. These traits or core factors are extraversion, agreeableness, conscientiousness, neuroticism and openness, and the suggestion is that they vary between people in ways that predict how capable of intimacy we may be.

It is somewhat controversial to pin people down to personality types and see some traits as more enabling of intimacy than others, not least because our behaviours or preferences are governed very strongly by context. Personality studies risk underestimating the impact of the conditions under which we behave well or badly, neurotically or feel open to experience. So I am sceptical of applying big-five theory to the question of who is more or less prone to good intimate connections.

That said, people are not identical and some are luckier than others in having stronger temperamental resources to draw on. The best insights in this regard come from John Bowlby's attachment theory. Attachment, for Bowlby, is a "lasting psychological connectedness between human beings" (1969: 194). "Attachment theory regards the propensity to make intimate emotional bonds to particular individuals as a basic component of human nature, already present in germinal form in the neonate and continuing through adult life into old age" (1988: 120–21)

What Bowlby discovered about the capacity to connect in infants and young children has been developed and extended to account for adults' capacity for intimacy too. The theory is based on the claim that we differ in our attachment styles in four ways based on two dimensions; the first of which is to do with avoidance and the second to do with anxiety.

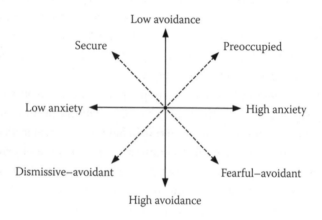

As the diagram here shows, this creates a range of possibilities that combine these tendencies. If you are low on both anxiety and avoidance you have a "secure" attachment style and are more prone to intimate connections with others. You are more likely to disclose private and important sides of yourself (verbally or otherwise), and are able to respond to similar disclosures in a way that helps the other person feel validated, understood and cared for. According to the theory, this style of attachment usually results from a history of warm and responsive interactions with relationship partners. Securely attached people tend to have positive views of themselves, their partners and their relationships in general, and will tend to agree with the following statement:

1. Secure: "it is relatively easy for me to become emotionally close to others. I am comfortable depending on others and having others depend on me. I don't worry about being alone or having others not accept me."

By contrast the statements that best describe the other styles of attachment are as follows:

2. Anxious/preoccupied: "I want to be completely emotionally intimate with others, but I often find that others are reluctant to get as close as I would like. I am uncomfortable being without close relationships, but I sometimes worry that others don't value me as much as I value them."
3. Dismissive–avoidant: "I am comfortable without close emotional relationships. It is very important to me to feel independent and self-sufficient, and I prefer not to depend on others or have others depend on me."
4. Fearful–avoidant: "I am somewhat uncomfortable getting close to others. I want emotionally close relationships, but I find it difficult to trust others completely, or to depend on them. I sometimes worry that I will be hurt if I allow myself to become too close to others."

Barriers to intimacy, unsurprisingly, arise in these non-secure quadrants: people who appear on the diagram above as preoccupied or dismissive. Those who are preoccupied are low on avoidance but high on anxiety. This leads them to push too hard for intimacy and thus push it away. Their expression of a desire for connection, laced with anxiety, can come across as needy or clingy.

Dismissive–avoidant people tend towards the "I don't need anybody" bracket. Bowlby calls them "compulsively self-reliant". They view themselves as self-sufficient and invulnerable to the feelings that come with close attachments. They often think less of their partners than themselves and can often seem defensive. They often suppress their feelings and get their retaliation in first; that is, they deal with rejection by distancing themselves from its possible source (namely other people).

People with a fearful–avoidant attachment style often have mixed feelings about intimacy: wanting it while feeling uncomfortable with it. They often feel negatively about themselves (unworthy) and their partners (untrustworthy). They also keep intimacy at bay and hide their feelings too.

In a different but relevant context the psychoanalyst Erik Erikson (1968) identified crises that predominate at different times of our lives. The early crises include trust versus mistrust at the start, followed by the tension around autonomy versus shame and doubt as a toddler. This leads on to the proneness to initiative versus guilt in childhood, and then industry versus inferiority in late childhood. As we move to adolescents we start to get closer to the tensions described in this book, namely identity versus role confusion for adolescents, and then intimacy versus isolation in young adulthood. Erikson also identifies later-stage crises such as generativity versus self-absorption in adulthood, and integrity versus despair in old age. He identified three conditions for forming and sustaining intimate relations in that crucial young adult phase, namely:

- a capacity for commitment – the ability to make a significant investment in a relationship "without fear of ego loss";
- a capacity for depth – the ability to reveal oneself, to involve oneself emotionally, to share oneself sexually and to air ones differences; and
- a capacity to maintain individuation in the context of pressures to fuse with another.

It would seem that a secure attachment style increases the chance of meeting these conditions.

For Bowlby an attachment style is not predetermined. That is to say it does not derive much from the usual suspects of genetic inheritance or from interactions with our mothers in the early years. Instead his cybernetic theory – borrowing from the way mechanical or biological systems can reset themselves in response to environmental changes, like a thermostat – describes an emergent phenomenon tacking backwards and forwards over time. According to Bowlby, we build an "internal working model" over thousands of interactions, which stabilizes eventually and guides our relationships with others in the future.

| | | Thoughts of self | |
		Positive	Negative
Positive		Secure	Preoccupied
		Comfortable with intimacy and autonomy	Preoccupied with relationships
Negative		Dismissive	Fearful
		Dismissing of intimacy Strongly independent	Fearful of intimacy Socially avoidant

I think both these characterizations, around anxiety and avoidance, express our ambivalence about other people; alternately facing them and turning our backs too. Hell is other people, as Sartre put it, but so is heaven, it seems.

While there is something instructive in looking at these attachment styles it also bears noting that they are not entirely permanent, unchanging states. Preferences and habits may alter over time. There are plenty of examples where the cool dismissive–avoidant becomes the preoccupied needy one when confronted by a potent enough audience. When Helen Schlegel had to face the disappointing morning after her kiss with Paul Wilcox she would have been hoping for more intimacy than he could give. She would have been preoccupied. Whereas when the down-at-heel and needy Leonard Bast, whom we shall meet again in later chapters, declares his passionate interest in her she merely laughs. With the power roles reversed she can switch from preoccupied to dismissive–avoidant. Intimacy is intrinsically relational; a new couple meeting for lunch each day during one week can each easily exhibit all four attachment styles over that time depending on the mood and what happened at the last meeting.

And when we move into the dismissive–avoidant or preoccupied modes this often indicates a reaction to the precariousness we sense in ourselves. Our helplessness is a fact, as is our dependency on others, yet we have developed ways of talking and behaving that will deny this crippled self-image. These ways of talking promise a sense of control, a magical freedom from our intrinsic defencelessness. Faced with helplessness, our language of bravery might tell us to "get a grip" when in fact the more courageous option might be to let go of the need to control the uncontrollable, neither walking away nor clinging on too tightly.

The need to trust

The currency we trade in is trust and credibility. No one wants to be a mug or credulous so it is easy to stay on guard. People often talk as though trust is based on a rational assessment of probabilities. But risk is built into it as much as uncertainty is built into any form of decision taking. The whole concept of trust is based on taking a leap of faith, and hoping the other will "tread softly". To trust someone is to give them credit, to suspend disbelief willingly. It means closing your eyes and baring your cheek, without peeking. And sometimes this requires a degree of courage. But without it the merry-go-round of playing safe keeps turning.

More to the point, because we are talking about a dynamic, relational process, trusting another person has an impact on them too. This is where intimacy takes on a moral dimension. To trust is crucially about a renunciation of control. As the philosopher Annette Baier (1995) observes, it is partly in trusting someone that you create the conditions under which the other person becomes trustworthy.

> This is partly because trusting people involves seeing them as competent and benevolent, and gives rise to optimistic expectations of response to the trust placed in them ... Moreover, by trusting someone, I give that person certain moral opportunities, for cooperation, generosity, or beneficence, for example, which she might not otherwise have had. Thus, when I trust someone, I help her exercise moral agency. (Miller 2000: 52)

There are no guarantees that trust will be rewarded in this way. Going back to *Lost in Translation*, as Charlotte grew closer to Bob she couldn't have expected that he would spend a night with the hotel's nightclub singer. And while she turned her heel after discovering this unpleasant reality the following morning, getting close to him was still ultimately a risk worth taking. The implication is that despite being hurt, she did not regret making the connection. Nor is that connection completely broken by his one-night stand; they slowly and painfully reconnect in stages during the next day, first over a dismal lunch of alarmingly unappetizing and unidentifiable dishes in a sushi restaurant, then when they meet outside the hotel during a fire alarm, and finally reconnect at the bar after that.

The only way to tackle insecurity is to choose to take the risk: to be brave enough to risk getting hurt. If both the avoidant and preoccupied attachment styles impede our chances of intimacy then the bravery required goes in both directions. When we tend towards the avoidant pole we need to risk submitting to the judgement of others, acknowledging the fact that "no man is an island, entire of itself"; whereas in the preoccupied mode we need to override our neediness and risk walking away. The unstable dynamic of intimacy requires identifying which way the pendulum has swung and being brave enough to push it the other way.

9

Solipsism and Imaginative Failures

If a transcription of our day's speech would make uncomfortable reading, how much more dismaying, perhaps, would be a record of our thoughts. For a moment she imagined how it would look. A mixture of memories, fleeting and prolonged, what-if speculations, idle observations, regrets – that would be its shape for most of us, and for most of us too, the leitmotiv would be ... Isabel paused, unwilling to reach a conclusion so solipsistic, but unable to avoid it; the leitmotiv would be me. It was that simple. Most of us, most of the time, were thinking about ourselves.

Isabel Dalhousie, portrayed here in Alexander McCall Smith's novel *The Lost Art of Gratitude* draws on the demanding conscience of a fictional moral philosopher to eke out this unflattering self-image. Normally we lack such self-knowledge. That is to say, we are solipsistic without realizing that we are. We are strangers to ourselves to a large extent. While much self-help literature suggests that self-knowledge is the first step to human connection, I'm not so sure. Our conscious self-image is the tip of an iceberg of unconscious work that maintains the self-deluding illusion that we are nicer and more in control than we think. Isabel, after all, had the omniscient help of a novelist, who was in a position to create a trick of the light. As E. M. Forster put it in his *Aspects of the Novel*:

> A man does not talk to himself quite truly – not even to himself; the happiness or misery that he secretly feels proceed from causes that he cannot quite explain, because as soon as he raises them to the level of the explicable they lose their native quality. The novelist has a real pull here. He can show the subconscious short-circuiting straight into action (the dramatist can do this too); he can also show it in its relation to soliloquy. He commands all the secret life, and he must not be robbed of this privilege.   (2005: 85–6)

I detailed in my book *Deception* that we will always come up against self-serving delusions when trying to see ourselves clearly. We do not have command of the secret life and are more complex than we like to appear to be. Mysterious to ourselves, we would do better asking an enemy to describe us than look in a rose-tinted mirror.

Therefore none of us consistently knows what we want, and should not always be taken at face value when we say we do. A nice example of this comes from the movie *Tootsie*. Dustin Hoffman plays two characters, a man and a woman. The man is an out-of-work actor called Michael Dorsey who is so down on his luck he takes the desperate measure of going for a major part in a daytime soap as a woman, Dorothy Michaels. He gets the part, is a great success (while keeping his true identity secret) and along the way falls hopelessly in love with Dorothy's co-star Julie Nicholls, played by Jessica Lange.

Dorothy establishes herself as Julie's best friend, keeping her tantalizingly close while ever prevented from revealing that she is in fact the besotted Michael Dorsey. One evening they are talking and Julie muses about how complicated relationships can be:

Julie: Don't you find being a woman is complicated?
Dorothy/Michael: Extremely.
Julie: You know what I wish, just once?
Dorothy/Michael: What?
Julie: That a guy could be honest enough to walk up
    to me and say "Hey, I'm confused about this too. I
    could lay a big line on you, we could do lots of role-
    playing ... but the simple truth is, I find you very
    interesting ... and I'd really like to make love with
    you." Simple as that. Wouldn't that be a relief?
Dorothy/Michael: Heaven.

Taking his cue he meets her later on in the film at a party, this time as Michael, and tries this approach, only to be rewarded with her drink thrown into his face before he can finish the sentence.

If perfect self-knowledge isn't the key element for intimacy, the *feeling* of knowing another and being known by them is. We are much better at seeing through other people's self-deceptions than they are themselves. Nevertheless, even knowing another person is a demanding and obscure task requiring some of those novelistic imaginative skills.

A few years ago I went to a talk by the philosopher Havi Carel who had just published her book *Illness*. It is a moving, autobiographical description of her diagnosis and treatment for a rare and, at that time, untreatable lung condition. Alongside her clear-eyed, insightful and unflinching account of the phenomenology of illness she observed how badly other people responded to her news: from indifference on the one hand through to what she called "pornographic interest", loaded into the blunt question "How long have you got?" At the end of the talk a friend of mine commented, "If she had twenty friends before the diagnosis I bet she has only half a dozen now".

Why? Because a test of an intimate relationship is responsiveness to the other's needs and wants. The reason people find it so hard to talk to the seriously sick or bereaved is that their needs are both strong and mutable. One minute she wants to talk about it; then she doesn't. One minute she wants to make light of it; then she wants to be serious or sad or angry. It is hard for a friend to keep up and to be faithful to those ever-changing contours. It is more typical to hit false notes and create awkwardness and disappointment. People fear what to say to the very sick because they know it can't match those strong and changing preferences. They are unsure about what would be helpful to say.

At the same time the intensity of these mutable needs might enhance the opportunities for intimate connection too. The conditions are set up well for light to shine through each of the four lenses I described in the first half of this book. So maybe the rider to the observation above is that those half-dozen friends are closer to her than the twenty could ever have been.

The difficulties we recognize in giving those *in extremis* a suitably empathetic response is only a magnified version of the challenge we have in showing empathy to each other in general. We are all as complex and varying in our needs and preoccupations as the very ill or the bereaved, only the story is written in lighter ink, and with lower expectations. The awkward gear changes are less obvious. When interpreting each other it is never as simple as that. We don't have telepathy. Instead we need the imaginative skill known as empathy.

Paths to empathy

In *Conditions of Love*, John Armstrong comments:

> People can be better or worse at seeing opportunities to make their affection apparent to the one they love. They can be better or worse at seeing what the needs or problems of the other might be; at recognizing the impact on

their own behaviour on the other. This has nothing to do with strength of feeling or intensity of longing. Instead it has everything to do with perceptual acuity and imagination. (2003: 29)

He goes on to say:

Our individual imaginative characters – the kinds of linkage we are sensitive to, our idiosyncrasies of sensitivity and response – entail that different people will be able to see more or less in any particular work of art. And we tend to like the ones we can see most in. (*Ibid.*: 97)

The quest for intimacy is more complex than appreciating art, since it is a dynamic arising *between* people, and requires regular changes of gear and imaginative iterations to achieve this attunement. We need to alternate between observing the other person's appearance closely and imagining their interior, as they must do for us, and thus, through successively approximating, arrive at a mutual understanding. The necessary skill to drive this connection is empathy. The philosophical concept of *Verstehen* comes close to this requirement of intimacy; namely, sharing the inner experience of another person, as they share yours.

In order to have an empathetic relationship with someone you need to combine three capacities: insight, sympathy and the skill to convey both understanding and emotion.

The first, *insight*, is the cognitive skill of intelligent observation that helps understand another person's thoughts, intentions and emotion tone – or at least provide the conviction that one has. While accurate knowledge is desirable we should not be fooled into thinking one can arrive at that detailed knowledge wholesale. People are so complicated that full understanding is too ambitious. The effective component is relative; it can be enough to understand someone better than others would do, or at least to enable the other person to feel reasonably understood in their own terms.

The enemy of insight is oversimplification. And yet common sense invites us to forget that. I once went to a management seminar and listened to gurus delivering a full day of unenlightening fare on everything from employee creativity to customer service. The bland abstractions were, like the proverbial apple pie, as uncontroversial as they were piously irrelevant. I found little to argue with until one speaker made a point about queues in supermarkets that stopped me short. He put to us the rhetorical question: "Who in this audience wants to make their life more complicated?" Of course the answer he expected was "nobody". To be sure, none of us wants, in pursuit of basic needs (such as a bar of soap), to be at the mercy of complex, bureaucratic red tape. We want to get things done, pronto. We want our soap, and we want it now.

It is no doubt a good thing that we have this capacity to simplify. We are pattern-makers and storytellers. But it is precisely because of this tremendous skill that we are very prone to its limitations. We routinely explain complications away "because this is the way in the world" and close our minds. We become weary of complexity and settle back into the comfort of simplification; and in doing so we pay a price. Intimacy requires that we ward off boxy explanations as far as is practical (although we may differ about what seems practical, of course). Instead, though, we switch our imaginations off and prefer to jump to conclusions.

But what Margaret Schlegel said of planning could as easily be said about oversimplifying. The quick and obvious-seeming path is rarely the route to empathy. Insight and simplicity rarely go together. How often do we close down the strangeness of our children by reducing them to mere "chips off the old block"? My younger daughters, Ellie and Charlotte, being identical twins, often encounter the laziness of people looking for peas in a pod. Every time we use phrases such as "we drifted apart", "boys will be boys", "it's just her personality", "it wasn't meant to be" or "I haven't got time" we are showing how much we prefer an oversimplified world as opposed to a more detailed look.

By contrast, intimacy requires that we sense the texture of another person's consciousness. One practical way to think of this is to listen to music or read something you've written with another person in mind. Imagine writing a story or a diary entry and then picture a close friend, a colleague, a parent or a literary critic reading what you have to say. In the subtlest of ways you can now sense what a friend might be appalled by in contrast with what might resonate for your father. What would make you cringe with embarrassment and what would make you feel proud, in whose eyes? Their imagined judgement of you can give you a clue as to what you know about them.

The second requirement of empathy is *sympathy*. The term was initially popularized in this context by Adam Smith and

David Hume. They used the metaphor of music to explain how the reverberations from one person could resonate in another: to describe the common vibrations that can make people attuned to each other, and which Smith called "changing places in fancy" (2002: I.I.i).

Sympathy is about the capacity to respond to another's emotion tone with genuine feeling, and to experience warmth or compassion. But there are various ways this can happen. Sympathy has different components, some of which enable empathy and some of which, surprisingly, do the opposite. One is mimicking the emotion in question, rather like twisting or tensing while watching a high-wire act. A danger of this kind of sympathy is that "emotion matching" can lead to "emotion catching", where you then inhabit too thoroughly the feelings the other is experiencing. She is homesick so you become homesick. This can pull away from empathy if it leads to too strong a reaction. I remember a friend telling someone else that her mother had died and that friend responding so strongly with her own mini-grief at the prospect that she too would one day suffer that loss that this became a barrier to connection between them. The worst of this is when you switch from being distressed for the other to being distressed *by* their distress. This was one of the many ways Carel was disappointed by people in response to her illness. She had to cope with their inability to cope.

The danger in this kind of response is focusing on yourself rather than the other person, or underestimating the differences between you. Instead one needs the imaginative skill to intuit or project oneself into the other's situation rather than reproducing it for oneself. We can learn some of this from lit-erature, as we shall see in Chapter 12. This requires imagin-ing how another is thinking and feeling sympathetically, but distinctly remaining yourself. This key ingredient requires that you are alive to what the other person is feeling without losing your sense of self or over-attributing how you would react in their situation.

Given insight and sympathy the third requirement is the expressive skill (whether voiced or indirect) to convey both that understanding and emotion in the right way, while being nimble enough to shift as easily as the mood. The right expres-sion, the one that doesn't hit the false note, as Carel discov-ered, may be in short supply. You might have the right kind of insight and sympathy but if you crash in with "you're just like me" you may well push someone away rather than bring them close. Sometimes it is about putting the right words in the right order (as Coleridge said was the task of poetry), some-times it is about tone and sometimes it is about maintaining an intelligent silence.

In Joseph O'Neill's *Netherland*, Hans is worried about a friend who has just been left by his wife for another man and is clearly in need of company. But his pride will not allow him to ask for it. Hans takes the initiative: "At a certain moment I asked Shiv if I could crash at his place. 'I'm too tired to head back,' I said. He nodded, looking away. He knew what I was offering." He says nothing more but the connection is made. As Hans admits about his tendency towards reticence later on in the book (about a different friend), despite his wife Rachel's finding it "weird":

[It] no doubt reveals a shortcoming on my part, but it's the same quality that enables me to thrive at work, where so many of the brisk, tough, successful men I meet are secretly sick to their stomachs about their quarterlies, are being eaten alive by their bosses and clients and all-seeing wives and judgemental offspring, and are, in sum, desperate to be taken at face value and very happy to reciprocate the courtesy. This chronic and, I think, peculiarly male strain of humiliation explains the slight affection that bonds so many of us, but such affection depends on a certain reserve.

Whether this affection amounts to intimacy, or perhaps leads on to it, is open to question, but what seems clear enough is that the affection would not be possible in the first place without that kind of discretion.

Some people become so self-conscious about being liked they neglect to focus on being good at liking or being interested in, actually caring about, the person they want to like them. They forget that the best conversationalists are good listeners, those who listen not just to what is being said but for the unspoken assumptions that lie behind it, with the skill to find common ground at either level. People like people who like them (skilfully): not needily or clingily, but with a knowing look and a genuine Duchenne smile.

The skills needed are not to be underestimated. The unempathetic or unimaginative, like Henry Wilcox, can never be vouchsafed those glimpses. Margaret Schlegel puts it to us as a choice:

It is impossible to see modern life steadily and to see it whole, and she had chosen to see it whole. Mr Wilcox saw it steadily. He never bothered over the mysterious or the private. The Thames might run inland from the sea, the chauffeur might conceal all passion and philosophy beneath his unhealthy skin. They knew their own business and he knew his.

Take Steve Coogan's character Alan Partridge, the idiotic talk-show host whose fatuity is perfectly described by his Abba catchphrase, "Knowing me, knowing you, aha!" Lacking every gift that is needed for connection, whether insight, empathy or basic curiosity, one can be fairly certain that the *aha!* moment has never been experienced by his interlocutors, who simply look on baffled at his antics. And oblivious to his limits he will seal the supposed connection with an outlandish, and anything but knowing, wink.

A truly knowing wink, by contrast, can create confederacy out of nothing if done skilfully. For sheer panache the best wink I have read about was described by Howard Jacobson, which he experienced at a dinner some years ago:

He winked at me once, from a couple of tables away, at a South Bank Show awards ceremony. You see, I remember the occasion. When Russell Brand winks at you, you stay winked. He opens up his face and invites you in to it. Everything is preposterous, the wink implies, but you should try it. It's entirely possible he was winking at a person behind me. No matter. I confess my susceptibility. I willingly registered the lewd comedy of its invitation.

In a conversation many years later Jacobson commented to me that Brand in his "callow youth" reached into this older, more experienced writer and pulled up his history and texture and made it his own. Jacobson clearly had stayed winked.

If the antidote to insecurity is bravery, the antidote to solipsism is imagination. It is the desire to look into others more readily than looking into ourselves. If we want to get close we need to pay attention. We need to develop our imaginative fitness in order to understand the grain and texture of another person's consciousness. We may not go to the extreme version implied in Joseph Conrad's line "I have never met a boring man"; perhaps only poets and novelists can have that kind of unflagging attention. But all of us can do better than we tend to if we listen carefully and let our imaginations run freer.

10

Wishful Thinking

It is striking how often people at a bar looking for a pre-dinner drink check to see what their friends are ordering first; instead of just deciding what to order they start looking to each other. Unable to decide we flatter sincerely through imitation. It's a trivial sounding example, but it indicates something interesting about our tendency towards safety in numbers.

Assertiveness of your particular needs and wants is as important to experiencing intimacy as being empathetic towards another person's. In hoping for an unrealistic fusion with the other we can start to lose the texture and grain of ourselves as we submerge to the group identity. Couples frequently kill off intimacy with this kind of convergence. They fall into habits of thought and action so calcified through repetition (a litany of "we do this ...", "we love that ...") that it becomes impossible to recognize the particular contribution of each.

In burying their own preferences, which they can now barely remember, they converge towards an ideal of the generic couple with few surprises. Highly reliable but estranged from their strangeness, they create a privatized form of common sense.

We are so preoccupied with the concerns described in the previous chapter – that is, coming across as solipsistic and inattentive – that we can at times go the other way. If only, as we might think, the poets and Russell Brand have the bold imaginative skill to leap across the chasm of separation, then this sets up an anxiety: that we will not be perceptive or skilled enough to follow the subtle palette of another person's rich interior. Faced with this anxiety we can be prone to over-reach, in which case the danger of being too solipsistic (lacking empathy), as described in the last chapter, is then replaced by the danger of looking for too much common ground and being too eager to please (lacking assertiveness). This is what I mean by wishful thinking. It is a tendency that is even further encouraged by a culture that conveys we might find safety in numbers.

> We are encouraged to believe, for example, that there are consensual objects of desire … The really frightening thing about desire is how idiosyncratic it is. We may desire people whom we might not like, or want, or whom other people might not think beautiful. So idiosyncratic is it that we want to pool this feeling, foreclose it, into consensual objects. The culture is encouraging the belief that there's more consensus than there in fact is.
>
> (Padania 2010)

Adam Phillips worries about the dangers of wishful thinking, or what he calls "magical solutions" that stop us facing
each other's helpless needs. This tendency, it seems to me,
can be a true barrier to intimacy. We saw in Chapter 5 that
to know someone is to understand their motives, desires and
needs. If Phillips is right then a culture that tends to pool our
idiosyncrasies will only succeed in making us strangers to
each other.

Why would we unassertively leave our needs to one side?
The reason is that although we may be shaped by our desires
(as noted in the quotation from Barthes at the beginning of
Chapter 5), quite often these desires, needs or motives are
not fit for polite company. Desires are not entirely within our
control and frequently push the boundaries of the accepta-
ble. When a man becomes acquainted with his unacceptable
desires, "he will be told, in short, that he is by nature greedy",
says Adam Phillips:

> He will discover, whether or not this is quite his experi-
> ence, that he apparently always wants more than he can
> have; that his appetite, the lifeline that is his nature, that
> is at once so intimate and so obscure to him, can in the
> end drive him mad. He may be sane, but his appetite is
> not. This is what it is to be a human being; to be, at least
> at the outset, too demanding.   (2006: 101–2)

We are much more confused than we sound because our
unruly desires, ones we only glimpse at times, need to be
shoehorned into a sane-seeming exterior. We cannot want

what we have because wanting implies lack; we may wish our wanting away, we may want to want the right things and pretend that we do, but this wishful thinking is not the same as insight. So the awkwardness of true desire encourages its suppression in exchange for more palatable glue, and this is why wishful thinking can prevent us thinking about our wishes.

Yet we cannot wish our wishes away as much as we pretend. We hide them, if imperfectly. We have unconscious processes that conceal, only partly, rather self-serving motives. This would not be so bad if we were aware of them and wanted to argue, but when they seep out unconsciously (and we explicitly insist on the contrary) they can create a wedge between people. I may convince myself I have your interests at heart but you might not quite see it that way. Picture a typical interaction between parent and child. The father has a "good idea" and is suggesting that his daughter takes up a musical instrument. But when she says she wants to play the drums this triggers a change in emphasis. Now he is suggesting the violin might be a better option. Despite feeling sincerely focused on the child's needs, the parent is sneaking in a few motives of his own. He doesn't want the racket of drum practice, or he doesn't feel his friends or neighbours would be impressed enough, so his advice becomes slightly polluted by additional motives. The child in turn is no fool; she can see the violin suggestion as being a little tainted and so discounts the advice to some degree. The parent seeing the child discounting starts to turn up the persuasive heat to compensate, which leads the child to discount even further.

In this case we can see how a slight initial mismatch in motives can lead to a significant wedge in the conversation, leaving the parent and child further away than they were to start with. The novelist Amos Oz talks about the family as the cradle of fanaticism. Parents, after all, like the fanatic, want to change you "for your own good".

In the pursuit of connection we can end up wanting much too much, much too soon, and the danger of too much wishful thinking is that it almost certainly comes at the price of identities suppressed and shoehorned into a false convergence. We do this because we know that the chance of intimacy without focusing on the other person's needs, without empathy, is nil. We look too quickly to safety in numbers, which may work well enough for the solidarity of a group, but does not sustain the more demanding expression of an assertive self that is necessary for intimacy between two. Where we should feel what the literary critic Harold Bloom called the anxiety of influence, we instead feel its comfort. Hearty convergence, while bringing rewards of its own, does not bring intimacy. Unassertiveness can be deadly. Instead we need the reading that Bloom attributes to "strong poets", those whose creative mis-readings put convention, cliché and derivative thoughts at bay, and thereby create the possibilities of new common ground. Without this kind of freshness we kill off the hope of crossing over to the mystery of another person.

Minding our language

The intimate revelations of young men, or at least the terms in which they express them, are usually plagiaristic and marred by obvious suppressions.

(F. Scott Fitzgerald, *The Great Gatsby*)

Communication is far more than a digital stream of information. Everyone is exquisitely sensitive to the stakes in a conversation: those changes in tone, that momentary unguarded glance. How we offer intimacy, how we accept it, turn it down, or bring it to a close all take skill. But they don't all take language. The unspoken, the non-verbal, are somehow more reliable transmitters, while explicit speech itself can often run counter to intimacy.

The reason for this is that adult language is prone to convention and cliché, shot through with self-denying manners and an awareness of dos and don'ts. Communication can be the enemy of intimacy because wishful thinking is so well afforded by the way we express ourselves.

By contrast, listen to how children speak: interrupting each other with abandon, demanding their needs are met and not taking turns. This is not to say the child's way enables intimacy either but it perhaps gives us an insight into how well mannered we have become and how far from honest talk we can drift.

Burying our particular needs and interests in generic veiled expressions, speaking is often "plagiaristic and marred by obvious suppressions". Whether through cliché or politeness, language can obscure more than it reveals about ourselves, and thus become the enemy of intimacy.

As if to avoid those numbing conventions we need to break the rules of politeness. Originality catches attention. Whether we fracture convention with an unfashionable view or shift gears to create laughter or surprise we need to find ways to avoid sleepwalking through a conversation. "I just called to say I love you", if said too routinely, becomes as dull as the repetitive bassline in the Stevie Wonder song in which it features. The merit of more unconventional language, by contrast, like poetry, is in its escape from literal meaning. It forces the listener to wake up, and to look anew.

Returning to *Howards End*, an example of this comes in the shape of Leonard Bast, a young man with a tenuous grip on a financial ledge as a lowly clerk. Leonard has hopes (if not the requisite assets) of self-improvement through reading and going to concerts. It is at one such concert that Helen Schlegel accidentally takes his umbrella, which leads him to track her back to their house.

When Leonard begins a conversation with the Schlegel sisters in their sitting room he tries to impress them with his reading but achieves the opposite effect. He keeps mentioning "beautiful" books, which leads them to mock his predictability. But despite his failed attempts to connect through his reading he makes a side comment that catches them off guard:

> "That's another beautiful book. You get back to the earth in that. I wanted –" He mouthed affectedly. Then through the mists of his culture came a hard fact, hard as

a pebble. "I walked all the Saturday night," said Leonard. "I walked." A thrill of approval ran through the sisters. But culture closed in again. He asked whether they had ever read E. V. Lucas's *Open Road*.

Said Helen, "No doubt it's another beautiful book, but I'd rather hear about *your* road."

The pebble that cracked the conventional conversation sent a thrill. Something new, overturning conversational convention, had happened and opened up a possibility for a closer bond. He describes his night walk and Helen asks whether the dawn was wonderful. "With unforgettable sincerity he replied: 'No.' The word flew again like a pebble from a sling. Down toppled all that had seemed ignoble or literary in his talk". Suddenly, by foregoing conventional talk, he is ennobled and emboldened by this genuine unexpected connection with these heroic women.

There are many conversational pebbles we can use to crack the smooth surface of linguistic convention. Leonard's unflinching honesty was one. Others range from very private revelations to targeted rudeness. The difference between conventional and unconventional language is like the difference between a fresh metaphor and a dead metaphor. While the latter has long since kicked the bucket (to such an extent that you can no longer see that bucket) the former has an irresistible freshness. It cannot be pinned down into literal meaning. These fresh uses encourage us to look imaginatively for patterns and shapes in meaning rather than fix on the literal particulars of what has been said. But as they die off from overuse, and once fresh-minted poetry starts to feature on Valentine's Day cards, we keep having to find new ways of creating originality. When Philip Larkin started his birthday message to the newborn Sally Amis with "May you be dull" he commanded our attention.

It is for this reason that couples so often develop their own private, conspiratorial languages. Rather than regurgitate conventional tropes, their abnormal discourse playfully steps out of logic into idiosyncratic wit or code. "Genius is to madness near allied", they say, but we don't need intimate couples to be geniuses when they get linguistically creative. A shared idiosyncrasy will do. They live on a linguistic margin, gathering up and describing unique experiences that keep others out of the picture; their collusive in-jokes and innuendo create that binding and sense of separation from the rest of the public glare. When the rest of us listen in it is easy to feel revolted. The language is too babyish or weird. Their unique language shrouds an exclusive relationship so as to turn the couple into outlaws. They idly ditch the rest of us. And where we look in and find them ridiculous, they in their turn, in a reverse of bathos, make it sublime, and the rest of us are going to have to deal with how left out they make us feel.

The attempt to find the words to describe an ineffable combination of feelings and insights will often prove counterproductive. Better to intimate. The veiled, the indirect and subtle are more often the hallmarks of the intimate communication. But if we do express ourselves explicitly in the hope of intimacy we know we should not be too polite about it. This also means that if we see uncompromising language as a way to asserting ourselves then we had better be ready to have an argument.

The kindness of conflict

Arguably the greatest impediment to intimacy that wishful thinking creates is the fantasy that we can have perfect agreement or, if not, that we can find common language and split our differences neatly. Our language, our self-knowledge and insight all have their limits and the attempt to overcome those can be self-defeating. By contrast we need to recognize our permanent divergences and try a little renunciation of convention and a tolerance of conflict.

In the novel *Netherland*, Hans and Rachel are having an argument about whether the US was justified in invading Iraq. She is vehemently saying not and Hans is uncertain and distracted, which only causes her to raise the volume.

She said, "I'm saying the US has no moral or legal authority to wage this war. The fact that Saddam is horrible … is not the issue … Think politically, for once. Stalin was a monster … Does that mean we should have supported Hitler in his invasion of Russia? …

I should have concurred. I knew better than to argue with Rachel about such things. But I was ashamed and wanted to redeem myself. "You're saying Bush is like Hitler," I said. "That's ridiculous."

"I'm not comparing Bush to Hitler!" Rachel almost pleaded. "Hitler is just an extreme example. You use extreme examples to test a proposition. It's called reasoning. That's how you reason. You make a proposition and you follow it to its logical conclusion. Hans, you're supposed to be the great rationalist."

As I've said, I never laid claim to this trait. I merely saw myself as cautious about my pronouncements. The idea that I was a rationalist was one Rachel had nurtured – albeit, I must admit, with my complicity. Who has the courage to set right those misperceptions that bring us love?

As the conflict threatens to change to the subject of them, and before it gets too difficult, Hans resorts to a collusive "misperception". Rather than take the argument out of politics and into something about how the two of them are with each other, whether they even know each other, he opts out. But the price of bringing us love in this way is precisely the kind of wishful thinking that leaves out intimacy. We are often too terrified, like Hans, of the conflict that might come from inconvenient truths voiced.

In her review of *On Kindness*, Mary Warnock comments that "the idea that enduring, reciprocal love or tolerance … cannot arise until both parties know the worst of each other and learn to accept each other as they are seems profoundly true". Adam Phillips (1994) comments relatedly that flirtation protects us from idolatry. The insight here is that to be too devoted to someone else can risk putting them on a pedestal and thereby putting them out of reach. The wishful thinking that comes with idealization or nostalgia creates a mythical variant of intimacy. The enemy of intimacy is not anger: it is sugar.

All relationships risk coating themselves in the sweet glow of nostalgia and quietly losing the granular understanding of each other and how we change. Intimacy requires an honest separation and is the opposite of submergence, which sometimes requires puncturing the sugary consensus with a salty barb.

But before I extol the virtues of conflict for intimate relationships it is worth recognizing how damaging it can be too. Couples interacting were analysed by the psychologist John Gottman in a longitudinal study that was able to predict the relationships that would ultimately fail with extreme accuracy (Gottman & Silver 1999). Essentially there were four danger signs, which he called the "Four Horsemen of the Apocalypse": criticism, defensiveness, stonewalling and, worst of all, contempt.

- *Criticism*. By this Gottman means the *ad hominem* attacks that tackle the sinner as much as the sin. Rather than criticizing the annoying habit, you turn the observation into a wholesale disparagement of your partner, using the absolutist language of "you always ..." and "you never ...", and putting their personality or character into permanent disrepute. "That was a bit selfish" turns into "You are selfish".
- *Defensiveness*. In defensive mode it is difficult to hear what is being said, and this can trigger various reflexes that can

be self-defeating. Typical examples are making excuses, rebutting the complaint with another complaint in return and finding one way or another to deny responsibility, "yes–but"-ing, repeating your own position until boring.

- *Stonewalling*. This is where you blank the other person by refusing to engage. Often disguised as merely trying to be neutral, stonewalling involves turning your back by changing the subject, maintaining a stony silence or just walking away.

- *Contempt*. This is the worst of the four horseman; the most toxic form of conflict. Worse than criticism, it is aimed at humiliation or at least disrespect. Contempt is an open sign of disrespect, involving eye rolling, lip curling, biting sarcasm, mockery or straightforward put-downs that can all be signs of revulsion or disgust. The carious reality is that things having gone this far have gone beyond recovery.

This is not to say successful couples always avoid these types of conflict, just that their presence is a yellow alert or worse. Gottman's research suggests that the continued galloping of these four horseman in a relationship can be used to predict, with over 80 per cent accuracy, which couples will eventually divorce.

Knowing this it is little surprise that we avoid conflict. We fear the expression of disagreement because it may reveal an unbridgeable gap. Hans understandably ducked this worry, but in doing so he only ignored the gaps in his relationship with Rachel; he didn't close them.

This point is made excruciatingly clear in Ian McEwan's *On Chesil Beach.* In this short novel we are confronted with a couple who never recover from their first-night agony of failed sex and a subsequent argument that destroyed them. Here is Florence's diagnosis of why she and her newly wed husband Edward couldn't contain a relationship-threatening argument that followed that disastrous wedding night. She runs off, after the episode, to the beach and he follows her. Their brittle conversation fails to repair the damage and things just get worse:

> She suddenly thought she understood their problem: they were too polite, too constrained, too timorous, they went around each other on tiptoes, murmuring, whispering, deferring, agreeing. They barely knew each other, and never could because of the blanket of companionable near-silence that smothered their differences and blinded them as much as it bound them. They had been frightened of ever disagreeing, and now his anger was setting her free.

This is the danger of what can happen when people go around each other on tiptoes, and each fails to assert their individual needs and preoccupations strongly enough. Over time, if a couple or close friends think too wishfully that they have more convergence and suppress their divergences, they will lose some of that muscular resilience that is needed to live with idiosyncrasy and argument. For intimacy to be created over a relationship we need to be accepted warts and all, as we say, rather than pretending the warts don't exist. And if we try to pretend then, like Florence and Edward, or Hans and Rachel, we risk a much more complete separation.

By contrast, the Schlegel sisters, whom we have encountered at various points in this book, show a similar ability to disagree sometimes violently with each other, and thus have managed a consistently intimate relationship together despite not finding such intimacy with others. They manage to hold on to conflict and thus to stay close.

By overcoming the temptations of wishful thinking and through taking the risk of assertiveness that might lead to conflict, we at least provide the conditions through which intimacy can be created. If, however, we succumb to what Phillips and Taylor call magical solutions we undermine the very possibility of intimacy in the first place. They comment on a feature of kindness that is equally true of intimacy:

> aggression itself can be a form of kindness; when aggression isn't envious rage or the revenge born of humiliation, it contains the wish for a more intimate exchange, a profounder, more unsettling kindness between people.
>
> (Phillips & Taylor 2010: 50)

11

Cultures and Contexts

Overcoming the three barriers I have reviewed in this part requires engaging with how we tend to deal with others. We need courage to combat insecurity, imagination and empathy to reverse solipsism, and assertiveness along with a tolerance of conflict to counterbalance wishful thinking. While none of these is easy to do, each can at times feel within our grasp. We should be careful here, however. Too atomistic a view encourages the thought that we are decontextualized individuals with the cognitive means at hand to control our own destiny. That picture, if taken out of cultural context, as so often implied or encouraged by the self-help industry, is hugely distorting, and falsely encouraging. It is a mistake to think that because you identify something in yourself you can thereby change it: attributing an attachment style to a series of painful experiences in your early childhood does not mean you can thereby shrug those off. More generally, the fact that something is contingent on a historical set of circumstances (such as the reason I speak English rather than Swahili) does not mean that it is thereby optional. As the philosopher Charles Taylor puts it, we don't get in and out of world views like a cab.

We are some way from the self-help picture that depicts us as free individuals making choices. Rather, we operate in a culture that powerfully shapes the options available to us. How, for instance, does the attachment style of "dismissive–avoidant" look when you think about the cultural norms of masculinity and femininity with which we all grow up? Western culture tends to discourage men from talking about their feelings, and also encourages us to control, and thereby overcome our helplessness. This set of forces, while hard to see on a day-to-day basis, makes us look like fish that cannot conceptualize the sea in which they swim.

We are pervaded, permeated, constituted by the cultural and ethical climate through which we move, and in that climate there are weather patterns that can disrupt the possibility of intimacy: unpredictable weather at that. The cultural, political, organizational or personal contexts in which we operate vary in the way they afford the possibility of intimacy; the minority are conducive, while the majority are not. Intimacy crouches into the small interstices of a public culture. Think of Bob and Charlotte in *Lost in Translation*, having to find their quiet escapes from the teeming, brightly lit world around them.

We shall return to the cultural disablers of intimacy in a moment. But even on a smaller scale there are more immediate contextual barriers to intimacy that are not susceptible to therapeutic remedies such as consciousness raising and looking within.

Time and place

The contexts that enable or disable intimacy reach all the way down from cultural norms to basic logistics. The immediate factors such as where you get to sit, what time of day it is, how much time you have, the physical layout can make a big difference to your chances of connection. Two students who catch each others' eye at the lecturer's expense need to be at the right distance and angle to see each other well enough. They are helped in their sense of exclusiveness by the crowded lecture hall, and their gaze is thereby intensified by the thinness of the thread connecting them.

Similarly the immediate contexts that fill marketing literature with the adjectives "intimate" and "cozy" provide the promissory note that the lighting (the alcohol) in our restaurant, bar, living room, bedroom will be the forgiving space in which intimacy can flourish. Marketeers have long known the power of offering the right context. The Soho House NYC brochure boasts: "There are three Playpen rooms in the House each measuring 325 sq ft. The Playpens are intimate and cozy featuring exposed wooden beams, light brown walnut flooring and vast banquettes upholstered in a funky banana leaf print". Yet most of the spaces we inhabit together don't easily allow the intimate or the cozy. More generally the institutions in which we live, whether these are family homes, workplaces, educational settings or the travel times in between, will often cultivate norms and logistical barriers that block intimacy.

Intimate encounters need more structural support than we like to say – more luck than judgement.

There's an adage to the effect that we choose our friends but are stuck with the family we are born into. But how much do we in fact choose our friends or partners? People talk of free and optional relationships, but that ignores the background factors of history and culture and circumstance that made them possible.

In a variant of the estate agents' mantra "location, location, location", psychologists talk of the *propinquity effect*: the not so surprising tendency for people to form friendships or romantic relationships with those whom they encounter often. And encountering the other person often will not be enough. It needs the right kind of time and space to refresh and renew a relationship. Holding down two jobs and looking after children with no help might well mean that intimacy would be out of reach even if it were a priority. Couples will often complain that intimacy vanishes after the kids appear; the relationship switches from face to face to something more like side by side.

Intimate *interactions* won't turn into an intimate *relationship* overnight. You can't make a close friend too quickly because you need to see their actions in different contexts in order to become familiar with their style and character. So many friendships fail to develop simply because lives don't overlap enough. And that too is why friendships are so important in our lives; friendship shapes the development of our personalities.

So often we see in films and novels depictions of connection thwarted by various barriers. The heroic overcoming of these barriers, whether family or tribal affiliations, cultural disparities, cruel intent or sheer bad timing, are the stock in trade of the "feel-good" ending. In reality, we don't often have such luck and often have to make do. Part of what is poignant about tearstained hellos and goodbyes at airports is how they have to find their way, because of limited time or enforced absence, despite the inhuman scale of the building, the harsh light, the noise and the crowds. People are forced to allow their private faces exposure in such an unforgiving public place. And those of us who stand nearby should try not to ogle. As onlookers we make up the public audience and need to show discretion.

Sometimes, despite the safe barrier of anonymity, we can cultivate a transient and, yes, intimate connection with a stranger. I was once on a very crowded bus standing near the priority seating reserved for people who need help. An elderly woman got on to the bus and set her path for one of those seats, its occupier having stood up and beckoned her over. The woman struggled through the crowds and, in order to avoid losing her balance, put her arm around my waist; this in turn led me to push a space open between people and, putting my arm around her waist in return, I then helped guide her to her seat, my arm interlocked with hers. It wasn't something obvious to others, I didn't take off my headphones and we barely acknowledged each other after she sat down. Just a half look, our eyes met fleetingly, almost expressionless

169

but knowing. Her vulnerability was clear enough, but one to which I needed to be civilly inattentive, and the moment that passed between us was unvoiced: nothing more than a half-nod of acknowledgement but a somewhat intimate moment nevertheless.

Barthes takes further this nonconformist idea of the comfort of strangers to celebrate the brief encounters of gay men in public parks and lavatories. And he extends this through the notion of the "trick" to account for the many ways intimacy can exist between those who know nothing of each other.

> *Trick* – the encounter which takes place only once: more than cruising, less than love: an intensity, which passes without regret. Consequently, for me, *Trick* becomes the metaphor for many adventures which are not sexual; the encounter of a glance, a gaze, an idea, an image, ephemeral and forceful association, which consents to dissolve so lightly, a faithless benevolence: a way of not getting stuck in desire, though without evading it; all in all, a kind of wisdom. (1981: x)

Wisdom, faithless benevolence, lightly dissolving, all might speak to the ephemeral yet forceful, maddeningly elusive and ultimately tricky character of intimacy and how we might see the glare of public culture as a barrier.

Typically the "comfort of strangers" refers to their ability to provide a blanket of anonymity rather than a feeling of recognition. We instead traffic in a world of "civil inattention" and where we connect it is usually to make a financial transaction.

"Gorgeous superfluity"

Money often estranges. On one level we might say that money is an enabler of intimacy. After all, only with basic needs for food and shelter met (*à la* Maslow's hierarchy of needs), one might argue, can we turn our minds to indulgent preoccupations such as intimacy. Listen to the ever pragmatic Margaret Schlegel on the matter:

> "But after all," she continued with a smile "there's never any great risk as long as you have money" ...
> "Money pads the edges of things," said Miss Schlegel. "God help those who have none."
> "You and I and the Wilcoxes stand upon money as upon islands. It is so firm beneath our feet that we forget its very existence."
> ... Helen and I, we ought to remember, when we are tempted to criticize others, that we are standing on islands, and that most of the others are down below the surface of the sea. The poor cannot always reach those whom they want to love, and they can hardly ever escape from those whom they love no longer. We rich can.

On the level that money buys the freedom to reach the ones we want to love and to move away from those we love no longer one can hardly disagree. Money certainly can buy the time and context in which to let intimacy flourish. But this also means that disparity in means or social status in various forms can create a cruel disparity in the possibilities of experiencing intimacy. Those who stand on islands have a huge advantage, like the character Fred Vincy in *Middlemarch*, frustratedly hopeful of a romantic connection with Mary Garth but who "had always (at that time) his father's pocket as a last resource, so that his assets of hopefulness had a sort of gorgeous superfluity about them".

The irony of Margaret Schlegel's message "only connect" is that it is only possible with people who have the money to provide, comfort, leisure, education and, crucially, status. The "rainbow bridge" she describes so eloquently that connects the prose with the passion, and without which we are unconnected arches, only seems to span across those islands that are so firm beneath her feet. Trying to connect with the submerged while standing on an island is, in *Howards End* at least, overambitious.

Recall the Schlegels' conversation with Leonard Bast. Forster introduces him as "grandson to the shepherd or ploughboy whom civilization had sucked into the town; as one of the thousands who have lost the life of the body and failed to reach the life of the spirit". While just keeping himself from the abyss, he has managed to improve himself through his reading and, while this has given him a path to the Schlegel sisters' sitting room, the undertow of their conversation is painfully informative. This is how Leonard felt immediately after their breakthrough conversation:

> That the Schlegels had not thought him foolish became a permanent joy. He was at his best when he thought of them. It buoyed him as he journeyed home beneath

fading heavens. Somehow the barriers of wealth had fallen, and there had been – he could not phrase it – a general assertion of the wonder of the world. "My conviction," says the mystic, "gains infinitely the moment another soul will believe in it."

The breakthrough he achieved, the pebble that cracked the Schlegels' own conventional complacency might well have been the beginning of a more intimate link. Yet the barriers of wealth had not really fallen at all. Because it was such an asymmetrical relationship he had ultimately no chance of intimacy with either of them. They had the power and position to condescend enough to find him interesting and, while thrilled by this nearly romantic encounter, he also, more soberly, knew enough to know it didn't fit with the rest of his life. "He did not want Romance to collide with the Porphyrion [the insurance company in which he worked as a clerk], still less with Jacky [his partner], and people with fuller, happier lives are slow to understand this": that an asymmetry of gifts or riches can impede the possibility of intimacy. To him the Schlegels as denizens of Romance "must keep to the corner he assigned them, pictures that must not walk out of their frames".

And the Schlegel sisters themselves, for all their expressed willingness to explore the suffering of others, the submerged, enjoy the gorgeous superfluity that sustains their expectations of themselves and each other. With assets of hopefulness of their own they themselves can provide a good example of a consistently intimate relationship with each other. Not constrained by a joint project, like a couple, they are free to express and explore their feelings and thoughts. And they have the intellectual and material gifts to do this with skill and subtlety and to be seen by the other as a rare compatriot.

And even when there is no financial disparity between people seeking an intimate connection the introduction of money is more of an impediment than an enabler. There is a well-known warning not to mix business and pleasure, or money and friendship. At a societal level we have the old distinction between hearth and marketplace. In *The Fatal Conceit* the economist Friedrich von Hayek describes the issue vividly:

> Part of our present difficulty is that we must constantly adjust our lives, our thoughts and our emotions, in order to live simultaneously within different kinds of orders according to different rules. If we were to apply the unmodified, uncurbed, rules of the micro-cosmos (i.e., of the small band or troop, or of, say, our families) to the macro-cosmos (our wider civilisation), as our instincts and sentimental yearnings often make us wish to do, *we would destroy it*. Yet if we were always to apply the rules of the extended order to our more intimate groupings, *we would crush them*. So we must learn to live in two sorts of world at once.

The point here is that the laws of the market if applied to intimate relationships would make them intolerable. A man selling his car to his closest friend may well be forced to choose what he values most in the transaction. Similarly if we try to place the loyalties, emotions and preferences that drive the "micro-cosmos" to the larger weal, running a country in terms of kinship, that would be problematic too. As some economists are fond of saying, "love doesn't scale".

We've seen in Chapter 7 how fraught power imbalances and the delicacies of exchange can be. Money and intimacy don't blend easily, which is why you peel off the price tags on the gifts you give. Moreover, money is how we acquire things rather than people and is the goal that helps us to forget the goal of human connection.

Anti-social media

Any discussion of intimacy needs to engage with those new technologies of connection that have pervaded our lives: a digital revolution that can equally be seen as a way either to connect or to keep people at arms' length from each other.

Our attention is now divided over so many channels. Using a smartphone at the dinner table, or laptops or tablets while watching television are in some ways increasing our productivity. The more fully we use what the new-media commentator Clay Shirky calls our "cognitive surplus", the more we can get done. But these distraction technologies also diminish our concentration on any one thing; and the nature and quality of that attention is diluted. When people sit together now, there is often a device in the vicinity with its quiet chatter of email or tweets threatening to interrupt. Friends are having lunch, enjoying each other, when one goes to the loo and the spell is broken as the other dips into the digital stream rather than reflect on the conversation in hand.

And when we move the conversation online rather than face to face a different dynamic is in play. Because the conversations can often be publicly witnessed the exchanges tend to be highly conventional and the display rules rigid and competitive. Just what is the right number of friends to have on Facebook anyway? (My, now 13-year-old, Anna suggests that I have some way to go!). In the world of Facebook, Intimacy according to the sociologist Zygmunt Bauman is being replaced by Extimacy (2012: 25 February 2011).

There are of course counterpoints to this view. The economist (and co-founder of the successful blog Marginal Revolution) Tyler Cowen, for example, in his book *Create Your Inner Economy* (2009) makes a bold case for the rise of new technology as a great enabler of intimacy. In particular he is a fan of instant messaging (IM) and other fast-and-loose interaction technologies rather than the more ponderous and deliberative email. His point is that the speed and informality of exchange in IM, tweeting or texting enables disclosures because you can feel more in control of where and how to communicate. According to Cowen they are therefore less guarded and more open than when they talk directly. People don't have to be too careful about tone when typing their messages to each other.

He also claims that these technologies enable us to frame our relationships with each other in a way that is helpful and enriching. When he is "friended" by a stranger on Facebook he actually feels a link to that person and if he ever meets them feels a warmer glow towards them. While he recognizes the limits of this view and wonders whether it is in fact a "friendship placebo", better named "acquaintancebook", he clearly sits at the end of the spectrum where new technology and genuine connections go together: "Twitter allows you to build intimacy with one group of people but not another, or in other words you can reach out and build intimacy with the people who are interested in you no matter what" (Cowen 2009: 76).

But consuming friendship in this way seems only to create what sociologists call "weak ties", not supplemented with real meetings. We can see the problem here when he tells us what is wrong with phone calls, by contrast: "I have a growing number of friends who ... avoid phone calls altogether. A phone call is a demand on you. A phone call is a chance to be rejected. And a phone call is a chance to flub your lines or overplay your hand" (*ibid.*: 72).

I do not doubt that phone calls or, even better, what tweeters call "fleshmeets" can be hazardous and unsatisfactory for all these reasons. But the very safety of online communications is why they are not suitable for intimate connections. The main reason why new media do not enable intimacy is to do with the controlled environment they provide. Yes one can make personal disclosures and be generous spirited, but what new media don't do is enable the openness to interpretation that real life encounters afford. All the recipient has of you online is what you choose to present about yourself. This is not conducive to the subtle interplay. And however slick and interactive the medium may be there is a delay in each communication too. It is not quite in real time.

Online we lack the means to weigh what Wittgenstein called "imponderable evidence" when we assess each other (2009: §§358–60). This:

> includes subtleties of glance, of gesture, of tone. I may recognise a genuine loving look, distinguish it from a pretended one ... But I may be quite incapable of describing the difference ... If I were a very talented painter I might conceivably represent the genuine and simulated glance in pictures. (*Ibid.*: 228)

The point here is that what Cowen sees as the beauty of online communications is exactly why they are not enabling of intimacy. They are too safe. Even with the freewheeling, near real-time exchange of IM it is clear that once you are expressing yourself through key strokes there are too many ways to conceal your emotional range and it provides too limited an option for others to know you better than you know yourself.

These "social media", while immensely helpful and productive on many levels, are, when we are talking of intimacy, somewhat antisocial. We are analogue creatures despite the digital stream in which we swim. For this reason there is nothing so old fashioned as out-of-date predictions of the future. Visions of paperless offices and three-day weeks didn't work out that way. Fundamentally we do not change that much. We were never going to live in glass bubbles without parks and countryside, and we were never going to live on capsules of protein and vitamins rather than food. And the internet will not replace our need to connect directly (although it may distract us from doing so).

In *The Meaning of Friendship*, the philosopher Mark Vernon has a chapter about "friending online" in which he shows up the limits of the digital age. As he concludes:

> a good lesson to learn would be that the internet is not so much a new forum for friendship, though it certainly brings more people within our orbit; rather it's best application for amity is as a tool for sustaining friendship. Virtuality may be liberating, as free as a planet whirling through space. But we are persons, and embodied persons too. Intimacy ultimately depends for its flourishing on contact in the real world, face to face. (2010: 120–21)

Even where people try to create real relationships on the web they are confounded by simulations. Direct experience of one another is necessary for having a dynamic and knowing interaction that might be described as intimate. Pursue an intimate relationship through these media, and we see a similar effect.

One aspect of new media that connects to consumer culture more generally is around the ubiquity of pornography. In her book *Living Dolls* (2011), the feminist writer Natasha Walter powerfully details how the commodification of sex through the welter of images that surround us has become a block to intimacy. She interviews a self-confessed porn addict who claims that for him sex is now a performance. "For Jim, the constant presence of pornography in his life has, he believed, threatened his ability to sustain intimacy. 'It has destroyed my ability to have intimate relationships. Its influence on my life has been so destructive'" (2010: 111).

More mundanely we can see some of the paradoxes of relationship forming in the online dating world. Fraught with vague hope, people, it seems, keep their options wide open, juggling multiple relationships with multiple people at the same time. Online dating agencies have discovered that keeping options open can ruin the client's ability to focus. The more they juggle the less time they dedicate to a particular person, and reduce the chance of a relationship. One of the biggest agencies, eHarmony seems to have solved this problem. According to Dan Ariely the author of *Predictably Irrational* (2009), they will ask you so many questions about your compatibility, and collect so many answers, that this leads to the claim that they don't have anyone who could match such a unique individual. And then after a couple more questions you discover they can offer up just one option. By giving you one answer they help you focus.

But there is another lesson we can learn from the online dating world that tells us something about our consuming selves more generally. Our hopes are vague. We are not well suited to specifying what we want or, to put it another way, we act as if anything will do to satisfy an appetite or to slake a thirst. This vagueness helps us to elide our desires into one big soluble want, into which the adverts can work their magic. So if you use fuzzy pictures and descriptions in vague terms this will make you more desirable in the online dating universe. People consistently fill in the gaps in overoptimistic ways. If I say I like music you think I like the same music as you. General convergence is easy when we are not specific. But the expectations end up being frustrating when they are both high and unformed. People don't learn, and are disappointed when they actually meet the person. And because they don't learn, as in retail therapy, they keep making the same mistakes and are just as disappointed each time.

Ariely makes much of a comparison with Barack Obama's campaign trail and why he has disappointed so many once supportive constituencies. He says that Obama has simulated the possibility of intimacy by staying vague about how to meet the people's hopes. "That hopey-changey thing" is so open-ended that everybody reads into him what they hope he will be and the only question remaining is "When do I get to sit down and have my first coffee with him to talk things over?" He may have campaigned in poetry; like them all, he governs in prose.

Intimacy is something we want in our lives but somehow, as Fromm said about love, we think there is not much to be learned about it. Our culture favours an emphasis on self-perfection, exchange and the satisfaction of consuming desires rather than developing our imaginative capacity to connect to others. Counter to the cultural norm we should reflect on our own imaginative capacity to find people interesting, rather than waiting to see if they just happen to suit us well.

Equal rights, intimate wrongs

The homogenizing tendency of consumer culture has an unlikely but relevant echo at a moral level, when we consider the age-old concepts of fairness, justice and equity. According to Fromm, equality used to mean the conditions under which we could develop individuality; the context in which we would treat people as Kantian ends not means. But he points out that in capitalistic cultures it means sameness, where "union by conformity ... is calm, dictated by routine, and for this very reason often is insufficient to pacify the anxiety of separateness" (2010: 15).

Intimacy has a strange relationship with equality or morality. Morality lumps while intimacy splits. Intimacy leaves everyone else out of the equation. The principles of equality, blind justice and democracy are about recognizing the intrinsic and equivalent worth of everybody, whoever they are. Intimacy moves in the opposite direction by singling out somebody and giving them special attention and interest. Intimacy is partial and differentiates. It is about treating people unequally, and about what we don't all have in common.

A father who reads each night to his daughter might also genuinely care about the poverty and distress felt by millions of unknown children around the world. Yet the intimacy with this one child will trump thoughts of the distant suffering of others. This can provide a barrier of its own. Our moral instincts link to a need for communion, belonging and a larger commonality, but our need for intimacy pulls in the opposite direction.

The philosopher Richard Rorty summed this up in the title of his memoir "Trotsky and the Wild Orchids" (1999). Trotsky signifies his commitment to the collective and his submission to larger categories such as solidarity and justice, while private ironizing passions such as for wild orchids told of his distinctiveness. Our texture and idiosyncratic preoccupations, when looked at closely enough, look like those of no one else who ever lived. This is the democratized genius that Freud gave to culture. The irony is that by democratizing our genius, that is, by showing that each of us has a peculiarly rich interior, we forsake our commonality. In a way our moral judgements are less relevant to our intimate relationships than aesthetic ones. The generalizing "golden rule" so often invoked by moralists, "do as you would be done by", is the enemy of the particularities of intimacy.

For all its moral ambivalence, there is a serious character-shaping dimension to intimacy. Our intimate experiences help to create who we are. Relationships forged over time shape our personalities and define what we are to expect of ourselves, good or bad. Our intimates guide us to becoming one kind of person rather than another; ideally they create the person we wish to be. And for this reason intimacy can be threatened when I have changed or you have changed, if we are both going out of line with each other. If you stop being my intimate it means who you are no longer satisfies my sense of who I want to be. I no longer like the person I have become in the light of our connection. And so to say at the end of a relationship "It's not you, it's me" is no consolation because this unwanted intimacy we've created means it is still as much about you.

Concluding this part we need to recognize that the cultural and psychological barriers to intimacy are formidable. Enlightenment advice encouraging "sympathy", "harmony" and "fellow feeling" such as those expressed in the writings of eighteenth-century sentimentalists such as David Hume and Adam Smith have been replaced by something shinier and harder for our times. This sheen of modern consumption has little room for the granular mess of real lives and the cult of idealization and perfectibility we see in a world of advertising makes it hard to inhabit those interpersonal spaces successfully. Phillips explains:

> There is a strange, magical idea that you can consume without digesting, that you could eat without swallowing, as though there were no process. ... it's the difference between the mother who needs to feed her child, and the mother who waits for the child to have an appetite and *then* feeds it. It's an absurd cartoon, I agree, but capitalist culture is force-feeding us whether we're hungry or not. What this means is that we never know when we're hungry, and we don't have the space to figure out what it is we want. It's driving us all mad.   (Padania 2010)

More generally, culture will repeatedly place the need for intimacy below the other trappings of fame, wealth, success, power and so on. Friends or partners become prizes that symbolize our marketability on these various dimensions. And conversation; genuinely reciprocal, disclosing, emotionally significant and generous spirited intercourse increasingly competes with the talk of the town. Given these and other impediments we have explored in this part, how hopeful can we be of finding intimacy?

PART THREE

Finding Intimacy

Donald Winnicott once observed that "a sign of health in the mind is the ability of one individual to enter imaginatively and yet accurately into the thoughts and feelings and hopes and fears of another person; also to allow the other person to do the same to us" (1986: 117). That is all very well, but he also celebrated the capacity to be alone in the presence of someone else, calling this a "most precious possession" (1958). The pursuit of intimacy, as we have seen, is fraught with paradox. Chapter 9 advises we should pay attention to others and Chapter 10 that we should pay attention to ourselves. Similarly, for Winnicott, to be irresistibly other makes a connection worth having, while threatening the possibility of connection in the first place. It is as though we need impediments if a marriage of true minds is to be worth having. So this sets up the worry that intimacy is in some ways a mirage: a mirage of true minds.

The barriers I outlined in Part 2 can all keep intimacy out of reach. And even without these various barriers the worry that intimacy will elude us is understandable because the lenses through which I looked at intimacy in Part 1, while enabling of it, all have their contradictions too. The *reciprocal* component requires mutual awareness and reasonably accurate knowledge of each other when attention is fickle and self-serving, and self-knowledge let alone mutual knowingness is such a challenging and changeable task. The *conspiratorial* element is hazardous both for the discloser, who may regret sharing confidences, and for the recipient, who can be a sucker for the sense of discovery that comes with revelation. Unruly *emotion* is hard to control, by definition, and yet needs to be expressed aptly if we are to connect to another person. If it is too controlled we will seem uninterested and thus peel away, but if it is overblown it can become a self-indulgent display that can push the other person away too. Meanwhile, the urge to be *kind*, rather than nice, can come across as condescending or requires a degree of sobering honesty that might well be read as cruel.

It is no surprise then that intimacy is in short supply or short-lived when found. There is no reliable map to guide us. So in the absence of maps, and the presence of various barriers, what resources do we have in our culture to help us explore how to connect more fully than daily encounters typically allow?

There are various places we might turn if we want to build on our chances of intimacy. Candidates include religion, self-help, philosophy, social science and the arts. Of these, it seems to me that our best encouragement (guide is too strong) comes from the arts. Most religion is limited, on my account, because it reasserts that misleading concept of an essential self. The treasure hunting and pearl diving is made all the more challenging when that self is something that exists independently of our bodies in the form of a soul. And the God's-eye view looks like just another form of wishful thinking.

Self-help literature filled with contradictions and overconfident advice seems limited too. Seven habits, ten pillars, twelve steps, may occasionally resonate but in essence they oversimplify human experience, serving up yet more solipsism and wishful thinking. As they say of diet books, if self-help books worked you would only need the one.

Social science and philosophy do provide tremendous insights into the human condition and help us to recognize how much more is going on than common sense dictates. But they tend to generalize when the insight an individual needs is particular, and specific and contextual. In this regard the arts have something essential that is missing from philosophy. I shall return to this point in the next chapter. Moreover, philosophy and social science are only instructive in so far as they *tell* us things, while the subversive power of the arts is to *show* rather than tell. Showing, it seems to me, trumps telling if we want to learn to live with each other well. And so it is through the arts – whether paintings, music, films or novels – that we can more readily find the clues to an existence that makes us more alive to our own and others' distinctive texture without offering the false promise of full knowledge.

And of all the art forms, popular or otherwise, the most relevant sources of insight (as opposed to answers), it seems to me, are provided by novelists. In his *Aspects of the Novel*, Forster comments that for the novelist:

> there is an affinity between him and his subject-matter which is absent in many other forms of art ... The painter and sculptor need not be linked: that is to say, they need not represent human beings unless they wish, no more need the poet, while the musician cannot represent them even if he wishes, without the help of a programme.
>
> (2005: 54)

The novelist however, creates "word masses", namely characters, their nature "conditioned by what he guesses about other people and about himself" (*ibid*.: 55).

Given that many of the challenges we face in hoping for intimacy are to do with knowing ourselves and each other, novelists, with their educated guesses, can offer a good place to look for insight.

12

Learning from Literature

Life's nonsense pierces us with strange relation.

(Wallace Stevens)

I remember I once saw a young woman across a busy bar while waiting to order a drink, soon after the birth of my first daughter, Anna. I caught myself noticing that this woman had a plain face with an awkwardly shaped nose and then I saw her again as her father might have. I imagined how he must feel when he picks her out in a crowd or when she comes through the front door, and my sense of her changed completely. I was no longer making a detached aesthetic judgement; I was briefly involved in a particular life with an imagined, loving history.

However, perspective-changing experiences, like having my first child, come in relatively short supply. This is where good novels can help. The Canadian psychologist Keith Oatley has devoted his life to the psychology of fiction. One of his classic studies involved giving subjects two versions of Chekhov's short story "The Lady with the Little Dog" (Djikic *et al.* forthcoming). The first was the story as Chekov wrote it and the second was a rewrite of the story as a non-fictional transcript from a divorce court. The second version was the same length and presented the same level of reading difficulty as the first, and the subjects' personality traits and emotions were assessed before and after reading each version. Strikingly, the people who read the original Chekov story showed a larger range of changes on both fronts, echoing the changing emotional landscape of the piece of fiction.

"I think the reason fiction but not non-fiction has the effect of improving empathy is because fiction is primarily about selves interacting with other selves in the social world," said Oatley in a recent interview:

The subject matter of fiction is constantly about why she did this, or if that's the case what should he do now, and so on. With fiction we enter into a world in which this way of thinking predominates. We can think about it in terms of the psychological concept of expertise. If I read fiction, this kind of social thinking is what I get better at. If I read genetics or astronomy, I get more expert at genetics or astronomy. In fiction, also, we are able to understand characters' actions from their interior point of view, by entering into their situations and minds, rather than the more exterior view of them that we usually have. And it turns out that psychologically there is a big difference between these two points of view. We usually take the exterior view of others, but that's too limited. (Flood 2011)

Literature is an empathy technology that provides various ways to summon up emotions and sympathy in ourselves, ones that the characters are experiencing, and might thereby increase our chances of noticing more, perceiving more richly and connecting more with people we might have encountered in life as alien to us.

Because literature helps us with perspective taking and empathy, it can have important political consequences. There are many examples, of which the most vivid is probably the abolitionist sentiment that was triggered by the publication of Harriet Beecher Stowe's *Uncle Tom's Cabin* in 1852. After that book it was harder to accept slavery and the Civil War led to its abolition in 1865: according to legend, Abraham Lincoln remarked to the author, "so you're the little woman who started this great war". And what is the likelihood that half a century later he could have been addressing that author so patronizingly had he also read the novels of Virginia Woolf?

Those political consequences can provide a more enabling culture in which intimacies between previously disconnected people can begin. This is why Shelley called poets "the unacknowledged legislators of the future". And the force of those particular stories, while operating in a political culture, can be hugely influential at a psychological level. Anyone who reads Huckleberry Finn might be thereby less inclined to see skin colour as a barrier to connection. Maybe after reading the

Schlegel sisters' failed attempt to connect with Leonard Bast we will have more resources to overcome the barriers of class, wealth and social status too.

The more directly relevant task of literature, for my purposes, is in its depicting of life in such a way as to enable those imaginative leaps. It can show us what we are up against, even as we know we must "only connect". In particular it can help us deal with open-endedness and obscurity and thus indicate the imaginative resources we may need to have any hope of finding intimacy with others. This requires developing what Keats called *negative capability*: that is, when one is "capable of being in uncertainties, mysteries, doubts, without any irritable reaching after fact and reason". This is a difficult state to maintain. With Coleridge (the target of Keats's critique in the letter to his brother in which this concept appears) we are more typically "incapable of remaining content with half knowledge".

Milan Kundera calls the novel "art inspired by God's laughter" (2005: 160). He contrasts *laughing* with *thinking* much in the way philosophers distinguish the particular from the general. The German philosopher Wilhelm Windelband, for example, focused on two kinds of understanding: the "nomothetic" explanations of science, which generalize over various cases seeking out patterns, commonalities and laws, versus the "idiographic" single case study, which focuses on the idiosyncratic details that differ in the particulars from any other – lumping versus splitting if you like. In psychology there is a concept of the "nomothetic fallacy", which is the brief comfort that can come from taking on a generalizing label. The patient who learns that his sadness is actually "clinical depression" might have a fleeting lift in mood as a result of falling under a label that contains the problem and may cure it. But this doesn't last since the underlying sources of pain, whether to do with relationships, history, neurobiology or social situation, will not have been dealt with.

The novel's chief contribution in this context is in resisting the nomothetic fallacy. As discussed earlier, our culture celebrates lumping over splitting. Even when advertising wants you to "do your own thing", that thing had better look like a lot of things other people want to do if what they have to sell will satisfy you. Digitally enhanced social media offering multiple interactions alongside the shiny promises of consumption only weaken our sense of the particular, idiographic texture that makes up individual minds, thus keeping intimacy further out of reach. For Kundera, by contrast, the novel "does not by nature serve ideological certainties, it contradicts them. Like Penelope, it undoes each night the tapestry that the theologians, philosophers [he could have added advertisers] and learned men have woven the day before" (*ibid.*).

> But it is precisely in losing the certainty of truth and the unanimous agreement of others that man becomes an individual. The novel is the imaginary paradise of individuals. It is the territory where no one possesses the truth ... but where everyone has the right to be understood. (*Ibid.*: 159)

There are limits to this reading though. While abjuring certainties and truth, Kundera has a rather doctrinaire tone that somewhat belies his message. His rendering, for all its salutary iconoclasm, still leaves the novelist with a somewhat God-like vantage point, even if laughing rather than lecturing. His focus on the quiddity and distinctiveness of human motives while avoiding the anti-intimate generalizations of mass culture still makes a claim to special knowledge in some senses.

In *How Fiction Works* (2009), the literary critic James Wood does rather more than Kundera to explain what the novelist can achieve with, crucially, a *partial* mastery of this second task. He says that literature asks the poignant question, "Do we exist if we refuse to relate to anyone?" while recognizing the crookedness of any such path to that relation. He explores the ambiguous space between omniscience and ignorance – some novelists have god-like control, while others say "I never know what my character is going to do next" – of what the characters' motives and thoughts might be, with the concept of *free indirect style*.

Close to stream of consciousness, this style hovers vaguely between the authorial or narrative voice and the character's own voice by using language that belongs varyingly to each perspective. An example of Wood's own making is "Ted watched the orchestra through stupid tears" (*ibid*.: 22–3). He says that while this is written in the third person the word "stupid" is not quite Wood's own. If it were it would be a straightforward put-down, but as it is partly Ted's it sounds more like self-consciousness or embarrassment. Why does Ted think his tears stupid? Is this because the music is sentimental? Is it just about being emotional in public? And how much is Wood hanging on to the word as author in order to create a critical distance from Ted? Importantly, we can't be quite sure. Woods says the novelist is a "triple-writer", working in their own authorial language, the character's language and the language of the world. The pressure of this troika shows up in the language of the world which predates the novel's own and "has invaded our subjectivity, our intimacy, the intimacy that [Henry] James thought should be the proper quarry of the novel, and which he called (in a troika of his own) 'the palpable present intimate'" (*ibid*.: 29).

What Wood is offering us in this refreshing take on literature is what it might be like to develop negative capability: that ability to live in mysteries that seems not only to be the task of literature, but the task of intimate connection too. As Wood puts it, "many of the most absorbing accounts of motive are studies in mystery" (*ibid*.: 100). The petulant method actor will often ask the question "What's my motivation?" She needs an answer if she is to find a way to inhabit her part convincingly. Yet true motives are complex, subtle, mixed and to some extent unconscious. We lose this point when we, like economists, are inclined to assume there could be a simple answer. And this is our task in the pursuit of intimacy. As we saw in Chapter 5, to understand someone is to understand their motives, and to look past misleading advertised messages and infomercials. This is not to say there is a pot of gold to discover, but only that without some grip on *why*, we are at sea. As Wood puts it:

> under the new dispensation of the invisible audience, the novel becomes the great analyst of the unconscious

motive, since the character is released from having to voice his motives; the reader becomes the hermeneut, looking between the lines for the actual motive.

(*Ibid.*: 113)

Negative capability

One of the tropes of self-help in particular and our culture in general is to say that we all have a responsibility to help ourselves. This is where therapeutic culture lines up with consumer culture in some senses. The solution to your difficulty in forming relationships is part of a pattern that is true of many others and is best answered by making choices: seize the day, take the road less travelled, give voice to the child within, or start developing new habits. But this advice is overblown. It trades on the understandable hope that we can fix problems and control outcomes and that intimacy is within our reach. Yet a brittle snatch at intimacy will vitiate the experience. The heartbreaking but in some ways redemptive counter to this claim is that there is rarely a straightforward solution that we can or should be rushing headlong towards.

Some novels can take us on a more oblique and, it seems to me, helpful path. Their major achievement, as they relate to intimacy, is in their ability to convey and re-describe this help-lessness. That is to say, there is strength that comes from recognizing the limits of the control we have over ourselves and over each other. Wood provides a beautiful example from Nabokov of how free, indirect style can help us inhabit this feature of other minds. The penultimate chapter of his novel *Pnin* has the professor, after a dinner, having just heard he would be fired, sadly washing up a nutcracker, which slips from his soapy hand, destined to break a beautiful bowl below the water. As the nutcracker falls from Pnin's hands "like a man falling from a roof", writes Nabokov, Pnin tries to grab it, but "the leggy thing" slips into the water. This is what Wood notices:

> "Leggy thing" is a terrific metaphorical likeness: we can instantly see the long legs of the wayward nutcracker, as if it were falling off the roof and walking away. But "thing" is even better *precisely because it is vague.* Pnin is lunging at the implement, and what word in English better conveys a messy lunge, a swipe at verbal meaning, than "thing"? Now if the brilliant "leggy" is Nabokov's word, then the hapless "thing' is Pnin's.   (*Ibid.*: 21)

Pnin's helplessness is thus shown, rather than told, and even transformed into something we can briefly experience thanks to Nabokov's restraint from his own eloquence. On Wood's insightful reading we inhabit partiality and omniscience at once. "A gap opens between author and character and the bridge – which is free indirect style itself – between them simultaneously closes that gap and draws attention to its distance" (*ibid.*: 11).

The more general power of this insight is to do with re-enchantment. The sociologist Max Weber borrowed the word "disenchantment" to describe the rise of controlling processes of rationality: processes designed to make the world predictable and explainable. The unfortunate consequence of this was a dilution of the inexplicable ties that bind us to each other. Literature can reverse this tide of disenchantment. That is to say, with sufficient skill the novelist can draw us into the life-like experience of helplessness that shadows our brave talk. And without helplessness, without the ability to tolerate ambiguity, a loss of control, bad luck, inconsistency, the opacity of motive, without understanding the particular ache of being lonely, uncertain and insecure, we are probably without the ability to make intimate connections.

If we return to *Netherland*, we have encountered already two examples that are relevant to intimacy: a quiet gesture and a quiet withdrawal. In the first, Hans makes an unspoken gesture to his friend in need by offering to stay the night: the connection is made while unstated. Whereas in the argument he has with his wife, Rachel, we see him duck the brewing consequences of their fight over Iraq and thereby keep intimacy at bay.

Netherland is a novel about the quiet bewilderment that sits uneasily amid the relentless din of certainty, whether around what to consume because our advertised desires are neon bright and clear, or whom we belong to because of the clubs we have joined, and the wisdom we have received. Hans cannot look after himself in these ways; his Netherland (or hinterland, or what Dostoevsky called Underground) is out of reach. His eloquent gaze on to the world is not met with the confident voice he might need to position himself within it, so he drifts. And this is why he cannot but observe the slow disintegration of his relationship.

If we play out Hans and Rachel's story we see a bit more. The relationship falls apart as they fail to realign their wants and needs, over the course of the novel, after the twin towers came down on 11 September and Rachel moves back to London from New York. On one of his twice-monthly visits to see her and his son in London, Hans realizes, passively, that things have changed beyond remedy, and that his wife is seeing someone else:

> Who is he? I said.
>
> She gave me a name. She told me, without my asking, that he was a chef.
>
> I'll leave tomorrow, I said, and Rachel gave a horrible little nod.

"Horrible" does for Hans what "thing" does for Pnin. Neither O'Neill nor Nabokov need be reduced to such imprecision, but their characters naturally do, blunted by helpless pain. Rachel takes Hans to Heathrow the next day:

> Somewhere near Hounslow, she began to say things. She gave assurances about my place in my son's life and my place in her life. She told me of the agony in which she, too, found herself. She said something important about the need to reimagine our lives. (What this meant I have no idea. How do you reimagine your life?) Each of her soothing utterances battered me more grievously than the last – as if I were travelling in a perverse ambulance whose function was to collect a healthy man and steadily

damage him in readiness for the hospital at which a final and terrible injury would be inflicted.

Even when he is about to lose his family Hans has little to say and even less to do. His defencelessness is part of the reason she is leaving him, and yet the fact of her departure cannot stimulate him to push back. Contrary to the fairy-tale trope he doesn't chase Rachel while riding a white charger, or prove himself by besting his rival in some kind of duel.

They do get back together again, but mainly for the bland reason that Martin (her lover) leaves Rachel for someone else. Hans willingly goes back to her, but without epiphany, without a solution. His helplessness is no less palpable, it just has become less of an impediment. It may seem undignified for him to return after her rejection but in one scene, as they talk to a marriage counsellor, we can begin to see why this is a hopeful cause:

> It was not the case that I'd heroically bowled her over (my hope) or that she'd tragically decided to settle for a reliable man (my fear). She had stayed married to me, she stated in the presence of Juliet Schwarz [their therapist], because she felt a responsibility to see me through life, and the responsibility felt like a happy one.
>
> Juliet turned her head. "Hans?"
>
> I couldn't speak. My wife's words had overwhelmed me.
>
> She had put into words – indeed into reality – exactly how I felt.
>
> "Yes," I said. "Same here."

This is not really an explanation, let alone a revelation. But it is a helpful reworking of the idea of partial resolution (without the heroic work of epiphany or even a project of reform) that might enable a reader to find options for intimacy they couldn't see before. The moral of this story (if there is ever such a thing) is not a conventional morality tale grounded in self-help. We can imagine the kind of advice: "you are carrying the open-ended wounds of childhood, and until you can name these and heal them your attachment style will always fall short of secure", or some such. In essence, "get a grip". As it happens, in this novel learning to live with helplessness is more to the point. In fact, by finding a way to see helplessness more fully and humanely rather than as a failure of masculinity, or a leftover disfigurement from childhood, the novel opens up ways to imagine different resolutions, despite the certainties that are the stock in trade of popular culture. Getting a grip wouldn't have worked in this case; self-help wouldn't help.

So the invitation here is to renounce control, or at least not to believe that control is always the way out of pain. I argued in Chapter 8 that the only antidote to insecurity is bravery, but the language of bravery has too long been associated with knights on white chargers, whereas sometimes the brave course is to yield. If we go back to the enablers of intimacy – the mutual knowingness, the secrecy and sense of exposure, the heightened feeling of emotion that is not willed and the kindness to be gentle with each other's fallibility – these are all ways in which we can link intimacy with vulnerability.

Returning to Wood and his hope for literature, we can see that it coalesces around this idea of incompleteness. He does all he can to weaken the author's grip (on voice, plot, character, consciousness and crucially motive) in order to give us a better set of resources for real, un-authored life. He believes that the ragged edged uninterpretability of human affairs needs to be reflected in the free indirect style that sits ambiguously between author and character, mingling the obscurity of motivation with "unconsummated stories" to create what he calls "lifeness". To put it more positively we need to be ready to be surprised by the people we think we know.

The limits of literature

Wood picks a fight with E. M. Forster, who, in his *Aspects of the Novel*, contrasted "flat" with "round" characters, awarding interest only to the latter. Flat characters for Forster do nothing for us because they are walking clichés, whereas round ones speak. Wood convincingly refutes this claim by recognizing how flat characters can move us obscurely. He says the telling distinction should not be between flat and round, but "between transparencies (relatively simple characters) and opacities (relative degrees of mysteriousness)", favouring the latter. Flat characters, Miss Jean Brodie for example, with their tag lines ("I'm in my prime", "you are the crème de la crème") and two-dimensionality, are often more interesting than round ones because we know so little about them; we do not need too much solidity or roundness to speculate about their motives. Less is more. Muriel Spark, who created Miss Jean Brodie, thus holds on to the opacity of motivation; Wood comments that "she was intensely interested in how much we can know about anyone and how much a novelist, who most pretends to such knowledge, can know about her characters". Jean Brodie may hide behind her tags but not entirely. Did she really have her prime? Does anyone?

Wood works hard to keep his authors from promising too much. And he is constantly on the watch for those who do. But even the greatest of them must in the end do so. It is overambitious to expect a novel to abjure completely the uses of enchantment. Forster by contrast resists both the imperiousness of Kundera and the over-ambition of Wood. While Forster loses the battle of flat characters he wins the war of words on what we can expect the novel to do for us when it comes to insights into each other. He knows that if we are only to connect we must put his own books down, and walk away from *Howards End* and the Schlegel sisters. While "the novel is an instructive source ... we should be careful before we get too seduced".

For human intercourse, as soon as we look at it for its own sake and not as a social adjunct, is seen to be haunted by a spectre. We cannot understand each other, except in a rough and ready way; we cannot reveal ourselves, even when we want to; what we call intimacy is only a makeshift; perfect knowledge is an illusion. But in the novel we can know people perfectly, and, apart from the general pleasure of reading, we can find here a compensation here for their dimness in life. In this direction fiction is truer than history, because it goes beyond the

evidence, and each of us knows from his own experience
that there is something beyond the evidence.

(Forster 2005: 69–70)

As Wood himself says, a novel succeeds in so far as it adapts
us to its conventions. So there is a limit to what he can try to
will it to do; the conventions of the novel, however enchant-
ing, still hold life out for us to inspect. And while he struggles
to move from lifelike to "lifeness" itself, there is a structural
fact about the novel that limits us from seeing it as life as we
live it. There is a writer and a reader after all. However subtle
and subversive the laughter might be, there is always a God
and an audience.

Literary Review's bad sex award provides a good reminder
of the gap between literature and reality. There is plenty of
excruciatingly bad sex around, as Florence and Edward
found on Chesil Beach, but there is something distinc-
tively toe curling about bad writing about sex. (McEwan's
short novel, it should be said, is an example of very good
writing about very bad sex.) We laugh so hard at bad writing about sex precisely because there is an author in the
bedroom nodding, winking or letting it all hang out for
an audience too. Bad sex is bad enough when no one else
is watching. But intimacy fundamentally goes with privacy
and the fact that there are readers looking in can make a bad
scene far worse. Writing that reminds us that we are watching, whether it is sex or anything else, does the useful job
of dispelling that disbelief we may have been suspending.
The awful truth for those of us looking for some sustainable

reliable connection in life is this: for much of the time, even when we need it most, nobody is watching; neither a creator, nor a reader.

Beyond fiction

While intimacy may well be novel's "proper quarry", we in the end know we have to put that book down and get on. Despite being an accomplished creator of successful and failed intimacies, Forster knows better than Wood about where to stop:

> Here we must conclude our comparison of those two allied species, Homo Sapiens and Homo Fictus. Homo Fictus is more elusive than his cousin ... He is generally born off, he is capable of dying on, he wants little food or sleep, he is tirelessly occupied with human relationships.
> (2005: 63)

We can pause with Forster here for a useful reminder that in real life we don't need *too much* intimacy. Despite my devoting a book to trying to understand it, we should not fetishize it; most of the time we are justifiably preoccupied by other things. And like a too knowing stare, we couldn't take too much intimacy if we tried. We may be complex unconscious universes crowded out by inner demons and better angels. Even if our taste for status, greed, revenge, *schadenfreude* and self-absorption battle against empathy, courage and self-control, we still most of the time have a surface reasonableness that may be just as valid for much of the time as Freud's "seething cauldron of desire". As we saw in Chapter 5, just because we have unconscious motives that shadow our external versions, this does not mean we need to parade them or fish them out so tirelessly.

It may well be that most of our subtle texture is not in view, but bad faith is not always so bad. By contrast, for Forster the novelist makes characters unduly sensitive to it:

> unduly in the sense that they would not trouble so much in life. The constant sensitiveness of characters for each other … is remarkable, and has no parallel in life … Passion, intensity at moments – yes, but not this constant awareness, this endless readjusting, this ceaseless hunger.   (*Ibid*.: 62–3)

In life we do not have such ceaseless hunger or such tireless obsession. Quite the contrary, yet we cannot turn our backs on intimacy completely. Even with moderate appetites, intimacy even if only to be experienced "at moments" is still a key form of sustenance. And the novel is ultimately no more nourishing to the reader than if it were depicting a fictional meal. The illusion of insight is not the same as actual insight since, as Forster concludes about Homo Fictus:

> most important – we can know more about him than we can know about any of our fellow creatures because his creator and narrator are one.   (*Ibid*.: 63)

206

While (the novelist's) characters whose secret lives are visible or might be visible; we are people whose secret lives are invisible ... And that is why novels can solace us, they suggest a more comprehensible and thus a more manageable human race, they give us the illusion of perspicacity and power. (*Ibid.*: 70)

Maybe Wood has answered Forster well enough by showing the co-creative work good novelists enable rather than attaining perfect knowledge. But there is nothing he can do to banish their compact with a judging audience; that illusion of perspicacity and power is still more comfort than we can find in life. Wood wants to claim "lifeness" for the novel but even this won't do. The limit of literature is not quite that, just there is no laughing god. Wood deals well enough with that, although better than many novelists do themselves. It is also that there is no judging audience. We are thrown up into the action in life and have no more potent audiences than each other, free to cheer or jeer and with no script to follow. We can't stand half separated from each other without consequences. Who said "life is not a rehearsal"?

If there is any crutch we can lean on then it is best supplied in fictional form. We do well to look into novels for a view of ourselves and each other. But the limit point of literature is just another reminder of the limits of wishful thinking more generally. In the end we have to live without their help too. In his chapter "People", Forster speaks to why literature is relevant in this way.

In daily life we never understand each other, neither complete clairvoyance nor complete confessional exists. We know each other approximately, by external signs, and these serve well enough as a basis for society and even for intimacy. But people in a novel can be understood completely by the reader, if the novelist wishes; their inner as well as their outer life can be exposed. And this is why they often seem more definite than characters in history, or even our own friends; we have been told all about them that can be told; even if they are imperfect or unreal they do not contain any secrets, whereas our friends do and must, mutual secrecy being one of the conditions of life upon this globe.   (*Ibid.*: 56–7)

13

In Good Faith

Bertrand Russell once commented that if we had telepathy and could accurately read off each other's thoughts it would initially be a disaster. People would see each other's unutterable little truths, which would poison the most comfortable of relationships. We wouldn't be able to bear each other. But over time, as these painful insights started to become familiar, we would begin to find a way to live with them and with each other again. We would acclimatize.

The awkward truth in his insight is that there is undeniably a gap between the barely coherent and somewhat indigestible stream of our consciousness and the way we frame ourselves to each other. If we could interpret anything, the biggest shock we might get is how little we figure in each other's thoughts at all, as we saw Isabel Dalhousie discovered, at the start of Chapter 9. But her conscious thinking is the tip of an iceberg of mental activity, most of which is never available for introspection (if she was an actual person). As we have seen, what is wrong with Russell's picture is the thought that these mental states could be read off in the first place: back to our buried treasure again. All understanding involves translation, from one mind to another. And this can't happen without loss, because the other mind isn't fully available, even to its owner. Russell's anecdote presupposes that those thoughts are legible in the first place. In fact they are a blurry melange: chunky crystals of meaning floating in a soup of feeling and association; like musical chords with their harmonics and resonances. We are mysteries to ourselves and so must remain so to each other.

In this book I have tried to describe four, somewhat fickle, enablers of intimacy, something Bob and Charlotte in *Lost in Translation*, whom we met at the beginning of this book, achieved so well during their brief encounter. They are:

- *mutual knowledge*, where the critical element is reciprocal awareness and reasonably accurate understanding of each other, along with a sense of exclusivity;
- *confidentiality*, the key features of which are disclosure or at least exposure and vulnerability, alongside a sense of discovery;
- *emotion*, thereby heightened, where the stakes are therefore high and to some degree outside of our control; and
- *kindness*, a benevolent attitude towards the other, based on respect and affection, and crucially trust.

An "intimate relationship" is one that contains a regular (or at least occasional) supply of mutual, conspiratorial, emotional and kind "intimate" interactions of this kind, and the hope for more in future. They all take place in a dynamic context that takes agility alongside a renunciation of a certain sense of control; the kind of control we can achieve only when isolated. This brings with it the discomfiting but redemptive fact that your identity is more available to another than it could be to yourself. To yield ourselves up in this way and to be met with kindness and insight is to feel truly justified.

But these enablers are complex and inconstant, making intimacy short-lived even when it arises. And even when they are all present they can vanish in an instant or indeed can turn into their opposite. Unfortunately, intimacy is unstable. It can shift into a counterfeit version without either person quite realizing when or why. That mutual knowingness can suddenly feel claustrophobic, the confidences exchanged regrettable, the emotion mawkish, the kindness patronizing. In *Conditions of Love*, John Armstrong comments on a depressing aspect of love that could as well be said of intimacy more generally.

> Among the most disturbing features of the experience of love is the way that it can be precisely towards those to whom we are most attached that we can have the most intense feelings of revulsion, criticism or desire to denigrate and hurt. (2003: 129)

Isn't this what can be searingly revealed on any given Christmas Day? There are no guarantees. Ambrose Bierce's *Devil's*

Dictionary captures many of the fraught themes in his definition of intimacy.

Intimacy (n.) A relation into which fools are providentially drawn for their mutual destruction.

Two Seidlitz powders, one in blue
And one in white, together drew
And having each a pleasant sense
Of t'other powder's excellence,
Forsook their jackets for the snug
Enjoyment of a common mug.
So close their intimacy grew
One paper would have held the two.
To confidences straight they fell,
Less anxious each to hear than tell;
Then each remorsefully confessed
To all the virtues he possessed,
Acknowledging he had them in
So high degree it was a sin.
The more they said, the more they felt
Their spirits with emotion melt,
Till tears of sentiment expressed
Their feelings. Then they effervesced!
So Nature executes her feats
Of wrath on friends and sympathetes
The good old rule who don't apply,
That you are you and I am I.

We can't be certain; we have to take intimacy on trust. We need to take a leap of faith and goodwill if we are to overcome the inevitable uncertainty of connecting to someone else. This hopefulness is the only antidote to Bierce's cynicism.

Worse still, even when we do achieve an intimate connection with another person we are exposed to another kind of loss. We can only guess at the shape of Leonard Woolf's disarrayed life after reading this final note from his beloved wife, Virginia, written before she drowned herself:

Dearest, I feel certain that I am going mad again. I feel we can't go through another of those terrible times. And I shan't recover this time. I begin to hear voices, and I can't concentrate. So I am doing what seems the best thing to do. You have given me the greatest possible happiness. You have been in every way all that anyone could be. I don't think two people could have been happier 'til this terrible disease came. I can't fight any longer. I know that I am spoiling your life, that without me you could work. And you will I know. You see I can't even write this properly. I can't read. What I want to say is I owe all the happiness of my life to you. You have been entirely patient with me and incredibly good. I want to say that – everybody knows it. If anybody could have saved me it would have been you. Everything has gone from me but the certainty of your goodness. I can't go on spoiling your life any longer. I don't think two people could have been happier than we have been. V.

(Quoted in Rose 1986: 243)

The grief memoir gives us plenty of examples of how time needn't heal too easily. In *The Year of Magical Thinking*, Joan Didion describes just such a relationship abruptly terminated. Her husband, John Gregory Dunne, died of a sudden heart attack at the dinner table one evening, and she suffers a grief that is an index of the deeply intimate relationship she had with him. A self ripped. She contrasts this experience with when her parents died, where she writes of a juddering of quiet, low-depth charges, but not of grief in the same way. She was still able to function when her parents died, whereas after the loss of her husband that first night she needed to be alone "so he could come back". So began her year of magical thinking during which she was deranged or forcibly rearranged. She struggled to give away his clothes because "he would need shoes if he was to return" (2006: 37).

Nor should we hope to recover too well from the loss of our intimates; the ability to recover too well implies that the relationship can't have mattered too much. There are, nevertheless, ways to live on in the face of such grief, but which have a more redemptive way of doing justice to an intimate relationship without denying its significance. We met Douglas Hofstadter with his swarm of bees at the end of Chapter 4. For all his representative idiosyncrasies, he forged a deeply intimate relationship with his wife Carol. Here he is on wrenching loss after Carol died of a brain tumour when their children were five and two. A few weeks later, Hofstadter came upon her photograph.

I looked at her face and I looked so deeply that I felt I was behind her eyes, and all at once, I found myself saying, as tears flowed, "That's me! That's me!" And those simple words brought back many thoughts that I had had before, about the fusion of our souls into one higher-level entity, about the fact that at the core of both our souls lay our identical hopes and dreams for our children, about the notion that those hopes were not separate or distinct hopes but were just one hope, one clear thing that defined us both, that welded us into a unit, the kind of unit I had but dimly imagined before being married and having children. I realized then that though Carol had died, that core piece of her had not died at all, but that it lived on very determinedly in my brain.   (2007: 228)

Despite all, the hope remains. We know that if we turn our backs on the hope for intimacy we will have diminished ourselves. Goodwill helps supply the ambition to leap the chasm, and not to live alone. The effort is everything. And even that botched near miss, with its undertow of hot shame, can generate enough satisfaction through its very daring to keep us addicted and hunting more. Goodwill can cross the gap of misunderstanding and poor translation. Good faith is located in an act of trust and goodwill, the feeling not of invulnerability but of mutually accepted fragility. Forster, who has urged all along that we must "only connect", has nevertheless been unflinchingly honest about this:

All history, all our experience, teaches us that no human relationship is constant, it is as unstable as the living human beings who compose it, and they must balance like jugglers if it is to remain; if it is constant it is no longer a relationship but a social habit.   (2005: 63)

We need something less and more than full confidence in each other if we are to experience intimacy. Something less is to deal with the fact that one can never know for certain: that in the middle of an intimate exchange your partner or friend could be faintly irritated by you, or just not paying attention (I heard recently from someone that the more she nods actively and looks attentive in conversation the more her mind has wandered); that when you think you're making music you are merely striking a series of false notes. We shall never know.

And something more is to realize that everyone is in this position; and that by combining imaginative leaps with the preparedness to be hurt and a generosity of spirit we can connect with each other as a matter of faith. There is always the risk we shall be disappointed or hurt by our intimates, or even that we shall one day lose that person. Yet there is also the redemptive possibility that we might "only connect", and feel, if briefly, joined to another person in mind and spirit: mutually accepting, revealing, uncontrolled and benevolent. And that moment of intimacy – that shared and forgiving sense of frailty – is to be cherished, and could yet come to be a fleeting but profound component of a life well lived.

Bibliography

Ariely, D. 2009. *Predictably Irrational: The Hidden Forces that Shape Our Decisions.* London: HarperCollins.

Armstrong, J. 2003. *Conditions of Love: The Philosophy of Intimacy.* London: Penguin.

Aronson, E. 1976. *The Social Animal.* San Francisco, CA: W. H. Freeman.

Bachelard, G. 1994. *The Poetics of Space.* Boston, MA: Beacon Press.

Baggini, J. 2011. *The Ego Trick.* London: Granta.

Baier, A. 1995. *Moral Prejudices: Essays on Ethics.* Cambridge, MA: Harvard University Press.

Barthes, R. 1981. "Preface". In R. Camus, *Tricks: 25 Encounters*, R. Howard (trans.). New York: St Martin's Press.

Barthes, R. 2002. *A Lover's Discourse: Fragments.* London: Vintage.

Baumann, Z. 2012. *This is Not a Diary.* Cambridge: Polity.

Beckett, S. 2009. *The Letters of Samuel Beckett 1929–1940*, M. D. Fehsenfeld & L. More (eds). Cambridge: Cambridge University Press.

Bierce, A. 2000. *The Unabridged Devil's Dictionary*, D. E. Schultz & S. T. Joshi (eds). Athens, GA: University of Georgia Press.

Bloom, H. 1997. *The Anxiety of Influence: A Theory of Poetry.* Oxford: Oxford University Press.

Bowlby, J. 1969. *Attachment and Loss, Vol. 1: Attachment.* New York: Basic Books.

Bowlby, J. 1988. *A Secure Base: Parent–Child Attachment and Healthy Human Development.* London: Routledge.

Bradshaw, P. 2004. Review of *Lost in Translation. Guardian* 9 January. http://film.guardian.co.uk/News_Story/Critic_Review/Guardian_Film_of_the_week/0,,1118548,00.html (accessed March 2012).

Brown, R. 1979. "Intimacy and Power". *Voices* **15**(1): 9–14.

Carel, H. 2008. *Illness.* Stocksfield: Acumen

Cowen, T. 2009. *Create Your Own Economy.* New York: Dutton.

Didion, J. 2006. *The Year of Magical Thinking.* London: Harper Perennial.

Djikic, M., K. Oatley & M. Carland forthcoming. "Genre or Artistic Merit? The Effect of Literature on Personality". *The Scientific Study of Literature.*

Dutton, D. G. & A. P. Aron 1974. "Some Evidence for Heightened Sexual Attraction under Conditions of High Anxiety". *Journal of Personality and Social Psychology* **30**(4): 510–17.

Erikson, E. H. 1968. *Identity: Youth and Crisis.* New York: Norton.

Flood, A. 2011. "Reading Fiction 'Improves Empathy', Study Finds". *Guardian* (7 September). www.guardian.co.uk/books/2011/sep/07/reading-fiction-empathy-study (accessed April 2012).

Fordham, J. 2009a. "Happy 50th birthday Ronnie Scott's", music blog, *Guardian* (1 October). www.guardian.co.uk/music/musicblog/2009/sep/30/happy-birthday-ronnie-scotts (accessed March 2012).

Fordham, J. 2009b. "Nigel Kennedy". *Guardian* (7 October). http://www.guardian.co.uk/music/2009/oct/07/nigel-kennedy-review (accessed March 2012).

Forster. E. M. 2005. *Aspects of the Novel.* London: Penguin.

Fromm, E. 2000. *The Art of Loving.* London: Harper Perennial.

Gilbert, D. 2007. *Stumbling on Happiness.* London: Harper.

Goffman, E. 1990. *The Presentation of Self in Everyday Life.* Harmondsworth: Penguin.

Gottman, J. M. & N. Silver 1999. "How I Predict Divorce". In *The Seven Principles for Making Marriages Work*, 25–46. New York: Three Rivers Press.

Hayek. F. A. 1988. *The Fatal Conceit: The Errors of Socialism.* London: Routledge.

Hofstadter, D. 2000. *Gödel, Escher, Bach: An Eternal Golden Braid.* Harmondsworth: Penguin.

Hofstadter, D. 2007. *I Am a Strange Loop.* New York: Basic Books.

Hume, D. [1739/40] 1985. *A Treatise of Human Nature.* Harmondsworth: Penguin.

James, C. 1983. *From the Land of Shadows*. London: Picador.

Jones, E. 1919. *Papers on Psycho-Analysis*. New York: William Wood.

Kundera, M. 2005. *The Art of the Novel*. London: Faber.

Lewis, C. S. 1966. *A Grief Observed*. London: Faber.

Lois, J. 2001. "Managing Emotions, Intimacy and Relationships in a Volunteer Search and Rescue Group". *Journal of Contemporary Ethnography* **30**: 131–79.

Marar, Z. 2003. *The Happiness Paradox*. London: Reaktion

Marar, Z. 2008. *Deception*. Stocksfield: Acumen.

Mashek, D. & A. Aron (eds) 2004. *Handbook of Closeness and Intimacy*. London: Psychology Press.

Miller, J. 2000. "Trust: The Moral Importance of an Emotional Attitude". *Practical Philosophy* **3**(3): 54–54.

Padania, S. 2010. Interview: Adam Phillips, *On Balance. BOMB* **113**. http://bombsite.com/issues/113/articles/3623 (accessed April 2012).

Phillips, A. 1994. *On Flirtation*. London: Faber.

Phillips, A. 1996. *Monogamy*. London: Faber.

Phillips, A. 2006. *Going Sane*. London: Penguin.

Phillips, A. & B. Taylor 2010. *On Kindness*. London: Penguin.

Pinker, S. 2007. *The Stuff of Thought: Language as a Window into Human Nature*. London: Allen Lane.

Register, L. M. & T. B. Henley 1992. "The Phenomenology of Intimacy". *Journal of Social and Personal Relationships* **9**: 467–81.

Reis, H. & P. Shaver 1988. "Intimacy as an Interpersonal Process". In *Handbook of Personal Relationships: Theory, Research and Interventions*, S. Duck (ed.), 367–89. New York: Wiley.

Rorty, R. 1999 "Trotsky and the Wild Orchids". In *Philosophy and Social Hope*, 3–20. Harmondsworth: Penguin.

Rose, P. 1986. *Woman of Letters: A Life of Virginia Woolf*. Oxford: Pandora.

Ruskin, J. 1869. *Modern Painters*, vol. 5. New York: John Wiley.

Russell, B. [1946] 1961. *History of Western Philosophy and its Connection with Political and Social Circumstances from the Earliest Times to the Present Day*. London: Routledge.

Sartre, J.-P. 2003. *Being and Nothingness*. London: Routledge.

Sennett, R. 2004. *Respect: The Formation of Character in an Age of Inequality*. London: Penguin.

Shirky, C. 2010. *Cognitive Surplus: Creativity and Generosity in a Connected Age*. London: Penguin.

Simmel, G. [1908] 1921. "Sociology of the Senses: Visual Interaction". In *Introduction to the Science of Sociology*, R. Park & E. W. Burgess (eds). Chicago, IL: University of Chicago Press.

Simmel, G. 1969. "The Metropolis and Mental Life". In *Classic Essays on the Culture of Cities*, R. Sennett (ed.), 47–60. Englewood Cliffs, NJ: Prentice Hall.

Simmel, G. [1908] 2009. *Sociology: Inquiries into the Construction of Social Forms*, vol. 1, A. J. Blasi, A. K. Jacobs & M. Kanjirathinkal (eds & trans.). Leiden: Brill.

Smith, A. [1759] 2002. *The Theory of Moral Sentiments*. Cambridge: Cambridge University Press.

Sontag, S. & P. Rieff 2008. *Reborn: Journals and Notebooks, 1947–1963*. New York: Farrar, Straus & Giroux.

Stendhal [1822] 1975. *Love*. Harmondsworth: Penguin.

Vernon, M. 2010. *The Meaning of Friendship*. Basingstoke: Palgrave Macmillan.

von Hayek, F. 1988. *The Fatal Conceit*. Chicago, IL: University of Chicago Press.

Walter, N. 2010. *Living Dolls: The Return of Sexism*. London: Virago.

Warnock, M. 2009. "Humanity's Gift that Keeps on Giving". *Observer* (11 January). www.guardian.co.uk/books/2009/jan/11/on-kindness-review (accessed May 2012).

Weiss, A. G. 1987. "Privacy and Intimacy: Apart and a Part". *Journal of Humanistic Psychology* **27**(1): 118–25.

Winnicott, D. 1958. "The Capacity to be Alone". *International Journal of Psychoanalysis* **39**(5): 416–20.

Winnicott, D. 1986. "Cure". In *Home is Where we Start From: Essays by a Psychoanalyst*, 112–20. New York: W. W. Norton.

Wittgenstein, L. 2009. "Philosophy of Psychology: A Fragment". In *Philosophical Investigations*, G. E. M. Anscombe, P. M. S. Hacker & J. Schulte (trans.). 182–243. Oxford: Blackwell.

Wood, J. 2009. *How Fiction Works*. London: Vintage.

Index

1984 (Orwell) 47, 58–9

academic articles 17–18, 44
aggression 163
alexithymia 97
alienation 26
ambiguity 16, 29, 198
ambition, of relationships 6
ambivalence
  about others 5–6
  moral 183
anthropomorphizing 25–6
anxiety of influence 153
Ariely, Dan 180, 181
Armstrong, John 139–40, 211
Aron, A. 18–19
Aronson, Elliot 67
The Art of Loving (Fromm) 70–71
arts 186–7
Aspects of the Novel (Forster) 136,
    188, 202, 203–4, 205–8
assertiveness 149
associations 62

atomism 165
attachment theory 125–8, 129–31
attention 115–18

Bachelard, Gaston 30
bad faith 205–6
bad sex award 204
Baggini, Julian 61–2
Baier, Annette 132
Barnes, Julian 51
barriers 119–21, 128, 186
Barthes, Roland 65–6, 78, 170
Batchelor, Stephen 61–2
Bauman, Zygmunt 176
Beckett, Samuel 10–11, 43
Being and Nothingness (Sartre) 46
Bierce, Ambrose 211–12
big five factor personality theory
    125
Bloom, Harold 153
books 10
boundaries, professional 53
Bowlby, John 125–8, 129

Bradshaw, Peter   16
Brand, Russell   146–7, 150
bravery   133, 201
Broadcast News (Brooks)   88
Brown, Roger   75
bundle view of self   61
Byron, George Gordon, Lord   23

capability, negative   192, 196–202
Carel, Havi   138, 143, 144
Carver, Raymond   23–4
Castaway (Zemeckis)   25–6, 50
categorical imperative   84
categories   31
caution   76, 124
certainty, contradicting   193–4
change   22, 165–6, 183
characteristics, of intimacy   44–5
characters, flat   202–3
Christianity   84
civil inattention   55, 73, 169–70
closeness   29
cloudy concepts   30–31
cognitive dissonance   67
cognitive surplus   175
comfort of strangers   169–70
commitment   129
commodification, of sex   179–80
communality   53
communication   154
community   61
competence, trust of   77
A Complicated Kindness (Toews)
    117
concealment   66–7, 152–3
condescension   111
Conditions of Love (Armstrong)
    139–40, 211
confidence   77
confidences   53
confidentiality   210
conflict, kindness of   158–63
connection   39–40, 153
connotations   24
Conrad, Joseph   147

consciousness   46
consensus   150
conspiracy   29, 40, 186, 211
conspiratorial lens   45
contempt   161
context   167–70
contradiction   65
control   113, 201
convention   11
conversational pebbles   156–7
Coogan, Steve   146
Coppola, Sophia   2
couples   79
Cowen, Tyler   176
craving   43
Create Your Inner Economy (Cowen)
    176–7
credibility   66–7, 91
crises   128–9
criticism   160
culture, effects of   165–6
cybernetic theory   129–30

Dangerous Liaisons (Frears)   71–2
dating, online   180
Deception (Marar)   67, 136
defensiveness   160–61
definitions   19–20
delusion   136
democratized genius   183
desire
    consensual   150
    for intimacy   10–13
    knowing   66
    unruliness of   151–2
developmental crises   128–9
Devil's Dictionary (Bierce)   211–12
devotion   159–60
dictionary definitions   19–20
Didion, Joan   214
disappointment   43–4
disclosure   69, 71
    see also revelation
discovery   21, 69–72
discretion   145

disenchantment 197–8
Djikic, M. 190
Doisneau, Robert 33
Duchenne, Guillaume 91–2
Duchenne smile 91
dyads 54
dynamism, of intimacy 140

Educating Rita (Gilbert) 26, 68–9
The Ego Trick (Baggini) 61
eHarmony 180
Ekman, Paul 89
Eliot, George 9
elusiveness, of intimacy 2, 5–9
embarrassment 98
emotion 186
    as beyond control 88
    as enabler of intimacy 87–8
    faking 91–2
    instability of 96
    kindness 210
    use of term 82–3
emotional intelligence 96, 97
emotional lens 45
emotions 45
    attitudes to 83–5
    categories 89
    and credibility 91
    expression of 91–4, 96, 97–9,
        100
    functions and effects 81
    matching and catching 143
    surrender to 94
    uncertainty of 95
empathy 138–9
    expression of 144
    and fiction 190–91
    insight 140–42
    sympathy 142–4
encounters 8–9, 98–9, 170
enmity 105–6
equality 182
Erikson, Erik 128–9
etymology 20–21
exclusivity 53–4

expression 144
extimacy 176
eye contact 52, 55–6
eyes 57, 71

faith 46
familiarity 29
families, and intimacy 7–8
family resemblances 30–31
farewells 98
The Fatal Conceit (Hayek) 174
fear
    of intimacy 10–13, 108–9
    of revelation 73–7
fellow feeling 109
femininity 166
fiction
    beyond 205–8
    and empathy 190–91
    see also literature; novels
finiteness, of intimacy 11
Fitzgerald, F. Scott 154
flat characters 202–3
flattery 149
fleeting intimacy 9
Fordham, John 26–7
Forster, E. M. 2, 8, 35–8, 136, 188,
    202, 203–4, 205–8, 215–16
four lens model 44–8
Four Weddings and a Funeral
    (Newell) 99
free indirect style 194
Freud, Sigmund 119, 183
friendships 7, 168–9
Fromm, Erich 70–71, 120, 181, 182

games 30
gaze 54–8
gender 166
genius, democratized 183
gift-giving 111–13
Gilbert, Daniel 97–8
Gladwellian Blink 55
Gödel, Escher, Bach (Hofstadter) 62
Goffman, Erving 29, 55, 98

goodwill 215
Gottmann, John 160–61
The Great Gatsby (Fitzgerald)
    103–4, 154
grief memoir 214
A Grief Observed (Lewis) 94
groups 60–61
Guardian 22–3
Gururumba 90

habit 149
*Handbook of Closeness and
    Intimacy* (Mashek and Aron)
    18–19
Haneke, Michael 23
The Happiness Paradox (Marar) 6,
    123
hate 107–8
Hawthorne, Nathaniel 109
Hayek, Friedrich von 174
helplessness 89–91, 131, 198
Henley, Tracy 18, 51–2
higher unity 60–61
*A History of the World in 10½
    Chapters* (Barnes) 51
Hofstadter, Douglas 62, 214–15
holding back 99–100
hope 215
How Fiction Works (Wood) 194–7,
    201–4, 207
Howards End (Forster) 8, 12, 43,
    101–2, 121, 130–31, 145–6,
    155–6, 163, 171, 172–4, 192,
    203–4
    kissing 35–40
Huckleberry Finn (Twain) 191
humans, Plato's image 7
Hume, David 61, 84, 86, 87, 109,
    143
humiliation 105

idiographic understanding 192
idiosyncrasy, shared 157
Illness (Carel) 138
illness, responding to 138–9

imagination 143–4, 147
imitation 149
imponderable evidence 178
impression control 46
individual knowledge 50, 76
Inferno (Dante) 40
influence, anxiety of 153
initial impression 56
insecurity 125, 133, 201
insight 58–9, 63, 140–42
instability 211
    of emotion 96
    of intimacy 29
    of self 21–2, 63
instant messaging 176–7
interaction technologies 176–7
internet 179
intimacy
    elusiveness of 2, 5–9
    as everyday 9
    and families 7–8
    fearing and desiring 10–13
    finiteness of 11
    fleeting 9
    in friendship 7
    loss of 1
    nature of 17–22
    short-livedness of 16–17
    talent for 9
    too much 205–6
    use of word 22–5
    voices of 22–5
intimate
    metaphorical extension 23–4
    use of word 22–4
isolation 25–8

Jacobson, Howard 146–7
James, Clive 112
Jones, Ernest 119
judgment 46, 75, 76–7
justification 123–4

Kahneman, Daniel 86
Kant, Immanuel 84, 87

Keats, John 192
kindness 104–5, 186
  careless 112
  of conflict 158–63
  as exchange 115
  and hostility 106–7
  idealization 117–18
  less as more 113–15
  paying attention 115–18
  and power 109–11
kindness lens 46–7
kiss, as icon 33
The Kiss (Rodin) 34, 40–41
kissing 33–5
  Howards End (Forster) 35–40
kitsch 95–6
Klimt, Gustav 33
knowing wink 146–7
knowledge
  individual 50, 76
  mutual 50, 63
  secret 66–9
Kundera, Milan 109–10, 192, 193–4

"The Lady with the Little Dog" (Chekhov/Djikic) 190–91
language 30–31, 57, 154–8
Larkin, Philip 157
Levin, Bernard 112, 115
Lewis, C. S. 94
lifeness 207
Lincoln, Abraham 191
Lish, Gordon 23–4
listening 145
Literary Review, bad sex award 204
literature
  and empathy 190–91
  limits of 202–5
  relevance of 208
  task of 192
Living Dolls (Walter) 179–80
loneliness 25–6
long-term relationships 79, 101–2
loss 214

The Lost Art of Gratitude (McCall Smith) 135–6, 209–10
Lost in Translation (Coppola) 2–5, 16–17, 132–3, 166, 210
love 49–50, 181, 211
A Lover's Discourse (Barthes) 65–6

MacEwan, Ian 162
Mad Men (Weiner) 113–15
masculinity 166
Mashek, D. 18–19
Maslow's hierarchy 171
McCall Smith, Alexander 135–6
The Meaning of Friendship (Vernon) 179
means, financial 171–2
media, rhetoric 2
mental associations 62
Middlemarch (Eliot) 74, 116, 172
mirage, intimacy as 185
money 171–2, 175
Monogamy (Phillips) 6–7
morality 83–4, 182
motivation 66, 77, 195
motives 67–8
music 26–8, 143
mutual knowledge 50, 63, 112, 210, 211

Nabokov, Vladimir 44–5, 196–7
needs
  paradoxical 6
  responsiveness to 138–9
negative capability 192, 196–202
Neruda, Pablo 29
Netherland (Joseph) 144–5, 158, 161, 198–201
newspapers 22–4
no-go areas 74
nomothetic fallacy 192–3
nomothetic understanding 192
nostalgia 160
novelists, as triple writers 195
novels 187–8
  see also fiction; literature

Oatley, Keith   189–91
Obama, Barack   181
Observer   22–3
On Chesil Beach (MacEwan)   162
On Kindness (Phillips and Taylor)
      107–8, 159
one-sidedness   50
O'Neill, Joseph   144
online dating   180
originality   155
others, ambivalence about   5–6
overextension, in use of term
      28–31, 50
oversimplification   141–2
Oz, Amos   153

Padania, S.   150, 184
Panopticon   58
Papers on Psycho-Analysis (Jones)
      119
paradoxical needs   6
paradoxicality   29–30
Partridge, Alan   146
paying attention   115–18
pearl view of self   61
personality traits   125
Phaedrus (Plato)   83
Phillips, Adam   6–7, 107–8, 115,
      117–18, 151, 159, 163, 184
philosophy   187
phone calls   177
Pinker, Steven   75
place and time   167–70
Plato   7, 83
Pnin (Nabokov)   196–7
poets   191
politeness   91, 155
pornography   179–80
power
   to hurt   124
   and kindness   109–11
Predictably Irrational (Ariely)   180,
      181
*The Presentation of Self in Everyday
   Life* (Goffman)   55

pretence   162–3
Pretty Woman (Marshall)   33
The Prime of Miss Jean Brodie
      (Spark)   202–3
privacy   77–8
"Privacy and Intimacy" (Weiss)
      77–8
private language   157
professional boundaries   53
propinquity effect   168
protective practices   98

rationalism   83
rationality   197–8
reason   83, 84
reciprocal lens   45
reciprocity   49–50, 105, 111–12, 186
Register, Lisa   18, 51–2
relationships
   ambitious quality   6
   constraints on intimacy   8
   renewal   11
religion   187
reputations   45, 66–7
respect, and reciprocity   111–12
Respect (Sennett)   111–12
responsiveness, to needs   138–9
revelation   40
   fear of   73–7
   limits to   79
   value of   72
   see also disclosure
rhetoric, of intimacy   2
Ries, Harry   44
risk   29, 73, 100–102, 124–5, 131,
      133, 216
Rodin, Auguste   33
Ronnie Scott's   26–7
Rorty, Richard   182–3
Rousseau, Jean-Jacques   86
Ruskin, John   15
Russell, Bertrand   105–6, 209–10

safety   57, 73, 75, 153, 178
Sartre, Jean Paul   46, 58, 130

Saving Private Ryan (Spielberg) 106–7, 108
secret knowledge 66–9
self
  instability of 21–2, 63
  reasserting 59–63
  views of 61
self-deception 67–9, 94, 137–8
self-disclosure 77
self-help 187, 196
self-mastery 83
Sennett, Richard 111–12
separateness 60, 120
sex, commodification of 179–80
sexual connotation 47
shame 57, 105–9
Shaver, Philip 44
Shelley, P. B. 191
Shirky, Clay 175
short-livedness, of intimacy 16–17
showing vs. telling 187
Simmel, Georg 54, 56
simplification 141–2
simulation 120–21, 179
skills 61, 98, 113, 140–41, 143–4
Smith, Adam 86, 109, 142–3
social media 119–20, 175–81
social science 187
social status 171–2
solidarity 61
solipsism 136, 150
Sontag, Susan 100–101
Spark, Muriel 202–3
The Sportswriter (Ford) 92–4, 97, 101, 102
stability, as illusion 21–2
Stendhal 123
Stockholm syndrome 106
stone-walling 161
Stowe, Harriet Beecher 191
The Stuff of Thought (Pinker) 75
Stumbling on Happiness (Gilbert) 97–8
submission 99–102
subtlety 15–16

superfluity 171–5
Swann in Love (Proust) 99
sympathy 109, 142–4
Symposium (Plato) 7

taboos 74
talent, for intimacy 9
Taylor, Barbara 107–8, 115, 117–18, 163
Taylor, Charles 166
technology 1–2, 175–81
telepathy 209
telephone calls 177
telling vs. showing 187
The Thinker (Rodin) 84, 85
time and place 167–70
Tootsie (Pollack) 137–8
torture 47, 59
traits 125
transience 169–70
translation, and understanding 210
trick 170
triple writers, novelists as 195
"Trotsky and the Wild Orchids" (Rorty) 182–3
trust 77–9, 131–3, 213
truthfulness 112
Tuesdays with Morrie (Albom) 11–12
Twitter 177

ultimatum game 86–7
The Unbearable Lightness of Being (Kundera) 95–6, 109–10
Uncle Tom's Cabin (Stowe) 191
understanding
  nomothetic and idiopathic 192
  and translation 210
utilitarianism 84

vagueness, of hopes 180–81
Venice 15
Vernon, Mark 179
Verstehen 140
vision 54–8

voices, of intimacy 22–5
vulnerability 73

Walter, Natasha 179–80
Warnock, Mary 159
We Need to Talk About Kevin
    (Shriver) 81–2
weak ties 177
Weber, Max 197–8
Weiss, Avrum Geurin 77–8
The West Wing (Sorkin) 124
When Harry Met Sally (Reiner)
    75–6

Windelband, Wilhelm 192
Winnicott, Donald 108, 185
wishful thinking 150, 151–3
Wittgenstein, Ludwig 30, 178
Wonder, Stevie 155
Wood, James 194–7, 201–4, 207
Woolf, Leonard 213
Woolf, Virginia 213

The Year of Magical Thinking
    (Didion) 214

Zappa, Frank 27–8